PLAZA CLUB BEVERAGE
10 FL. OZ.
Orange-Crush Soda
TALLY-HO BEVERAGES
LEMMY Delicious LEMONADE MADE WITH Real LEMON JUICE
LAMMO Beverages
HARMONY CLUB BEVERAGES
GATOR BEVERAGES
CHIEF WASHAKIE BEVERAGE
BEVERAGES
FROSTY BEVERAGES
MOONSHI
Vitamin Enriched
OLD STAND-BY BEVERAGES
Sour Puss
Glacier BEVERAGES
QUALITY BEVERAGES
Life BEVERAGES
Capitol BEVERAGES
CHIEF BEVERAGES
Chief Muskogee FINE FLAVORS
LEOMINSTER Home BEVERAGES
PLAYERS
STONE MOUNTAIN BEVERAGES
Virginia Dare QUALITY BEVERAGE
Uncle Tom's ROOT BEER FAMOUS for FLOATS
WESTERN BEVERAGES
LITTLE TOM beverages
AMERICA'S "THIRST" CHOICE Sparkling LIFE A BEVERAGE
REFRESHING-COOLING-SATISFYING
COLONIAL BEVERAGES
HUSKER A Champion in Flavor
LaFAYETTE Beverages
K.C. BEVERAGES KIT CARSON LOVE
ZEEH'S BEVERAGES
ZEEH'S BOTTLING WORKS KINGSTON, N.Y.
UNCLE SAM BEVERAGES
CONTENTS 7 OUNCES SEAPORT BOTTLING WORKS HOUSTON, TEXAS
CONTENTS 7 FL. OZS. Visniak SATURN VISNIAK, INC. BUFFALO NEW YORK
LITTLE JOE 8 FLUID OUNCES
Sweetie
YOSEMITE BEVERAGES
RED DEER BEVERAGES
"GOOD TASTE IN DRINKS" ALL-AMERICA BEVERAGES Lead the Field ALL-WAYS
CHICO SPARKLING BEVERAGES
Naturally Refreshing wigwam Fruit Beverages
TRU-Ade Not Carbonated
ZEISLER Delicious Refreshing Beverages
Sun Valley ORANGE
SPRAY LOCKHART BEVERAGES
WHITE LIGHT-NIN'
MOTHER PRIDE ROOT BEER
Sunny Side
HEEP GOOD BEVERAGES
Lamport BEVERAGE CO.
POPS it's time in ROOT BEER
TASTEE SUNTEX BEVERAGES Quality Supreme
HI-DIVE DIP IN THE DEEP
SOUTHERN MAID
SUN FLOWER BEVERAGES
TRICK TREAT 7 FL. OZS.
Washington
COUNTRY-MUSIC BEVERAGES
Cumberland Valley Beverages
the drink... of the DESERT Desert Beverage
Sun Flower BEVERAGES 12 FL. OZS.
St. Helens BEVERAGES Delicious Healthful
PELICAN BEVERAGES
RICH IN DEXTROSE Swanee BEVERAGES
SQUEEZE REG. U.S. PAT. OFF. MIN CONTENTS 10 FL. OZS.
Little Joe 7 FL. OZS.
HORNET BRAND BEVERAGES
DUNN'S BEVERAGE
DRINK EIGHT 8 BALL THE BIG FAVORITE
FAVORITE
ARCTIC BEVERAGES
ASPINOCK BEVERAGES
A-TREAT Premium BEVERAGES
INDIAN MOUND SPRINGS QUALITY BEVERAGES ACE OF THEM ALL CONTENTS 7 FL. OZ.
SPRINGTIME ANYTIME 7 FL. OZS.
CHESTER CLUB Quality BEVERAGES
LAND-O-LAKES BEVERAGES
LIFT Beverage
CASCADE BEVERAGE CO. WENATCHEE, WASH.
ICY I-C REFRESHING BEVERAGES
Sun Rise BEVERAGES
It's a Lindy BEVERAGE
Tecumseh BEVERAGES
LOG CABIN BEVERAGE
Peter Pan DELICIOUS-REFRESHING
Lake Tahoe CLUB SODA
The CHAMP of THIRST QUENCHERS
MANATAUG BEVERAGES MARBLEHEAD BOTTLING MARBLEHEAD, MASS.
MINNESOTA PAUL BUNYAN'S PLAYGROUND

Printed
in USA

Soda Pop!

From Miracle Medicine
to Pop Culture

By
Michael Karl Witzel
and Gyvel Young-Witzel

TOWN
SQUARE
BOOKS
an imprint of Voyageur Press

Dedication

In memory of my mother . . .

Endpapers: Applied color labels (ACL) were first used in 1934 as an alternative to identifying bottles with paper labels or embossing. This array shows only a small portion of the numerous regional and national brands of soda pop that flourished throughout North America. *Author*

Page 1: A 1909 Coca-Cola calendar girl enjoying a cold one. *Courtesy of The Coca-Cola Company*

Page 2: Movie star Paulette Goddard models the 1947 Royal Crown soda. *Author's Collection*

Page 3: A 1899 Moxie Bottle Wagon. *Courtesy of Frank N. Potter*

Facing page: Moxie Boy, circa 1921. "Meet the eye was exactly what this poster did. On it, was the picture of a handsome young man pointing. A bit of a smile was on his lips but those eyes were dead serious. He made girls blush and boys scuff and push their hands deeper into their pockets—where they just might find a nickel or two for some Moxie." Frank Potter, *The Moxie Mystique*. *Courtesy of Frank N. Potter*

Edited by Michael Dregni
Illustrations edited by Danielle J. Ibister and Michael Dregni
Designed by Andrea Rud
Printed in China

98   99   00   01   02   5   4   3   2   1

Library of Congress Cataloging-in-Publication Data
Witzel, Michael Karl, 1960–
        Soda pop! : from miracle medicine to pop culture / Michael Karl Witzel, Gyvel Young-Witzel.
                p.   cm.
        Includes bibliographical references and index.
        ISBN 0-89658-326-0
        1. Carbonated beverages. I. Young-Witzel, Gyvel, 1948– II. Title.
    TP630.W577 1998
    641.8'75—dc21   97-26702
                                            CIP

A Town Square Book
Published by Voyageur Press, Inc.
123 North Second Street, P.O. Box 338, Stillwater, MN 55082 U.S.A.
612-430-2210, fax 612-430-2211

Educators, fundraisers, premium and gift buyers, publicists, and marketing managers: Looking for creative products and new sales ideas? Voyageur Press books are available at special discounts when purchased in quantities, and special editions can be created to your specifications. For details contact the marketing department at 800-888-9653.

"Coca-Cola" and the Dynamic Ribbon device are registered trademarks of The Coca-Cola Company.

Contents

The bottle that made "pop," circa 1903

This style of heavy green glass, embossed bottle that featured the handy Hutchinson stopper were used to bottle flavored sodas and gave the drink its slang name of "pop." Charles Hutchinson patented his spring soda-bottle stopper in 1897 and used a loop of heavy wire and a stopper gasket: The thick wire acted like a spring and protruded above the neck. The gasket went through the neck and down into the bottle. After the bottle was filled with drink, the gasket was pulled up by the wire to make the seal. To open the bottle, one gave the stopper a swift slap with the palm of the hand. When the gasket pushed through, the pressure release created a distinct "pop" sound, and that's how carbonated drinks became known as soda pop. This 1903 bottle from the Dublin Bottling Works in Dublin, Texas, was once filled with Dr Pepper. *Author/Courtesy of the Dr Pepper Museum, Waco, Texas*

Acknowledgments

Our thanks to the following people and institutions, listed in alphabetical order, without whom this book would have been possible: Jennifer Andrews, public relations officer, Cadbury Schweppes p.l.c., London, England; Rebecca A. Berkley for her photographic research; Martin Cable, former manager of Stan's Drive-In; Cadbury Schweppes Public Limited Company, London, England; Lisa Berger Carter, associate coordinator of Rights and Reproductions, The New-York Historical Society, New York, New York; Marie Cavanagh, director of Information Services, National Soft Drink Association, Washington, D. C.; Chicago Historical Society, Chicago, Illinois; The Coca-Cola Company, Atlanta, Georgia; CoolStock American Icons Collection; Barry and JoAnn Darlington, Kansas City, Missouri; Michael Dregni, editorial director, Voyageur Press, Stillwater, Minnesota; Dr Pepper/Cadbury North America, Dallas, Texas; Jim and Mary Edds, Kansas City, Missouri; David Egner, Public Relations Department, Pepsi-Cola Company, Somers, New York; Mark Foster, Pepsi-Cola Meeting Services, Pepsi-Cola Company, Somers, New York; Gene Fowler, author of *Crazy Water*, Austin, Texas; Jim Foster, curator, Texas/Dallas History & Archives Division, Dallas Public Library, Dallas, Texas; Jacqueline F. Graci, Millis Massachusetts Historical Commission, Millis, Massachusetts; Millard B. Grimes, publisher and editor, *Georgia Trend* magazine, Athens, Georgia; Holly H. Hallanan, The George S. Bolster Collection of the Historical Society of Saratoga Springs, Saratoga Springs, New York; Gordon Harper, The Design Studio, Cadbury Limited, Bournville, Birmingham, England; Wendy Haynes, coordinator of Rights and Reproductions, The New-York Historical Society, New York, New York; Imagers, Digital Production Center, Atlanta, Georgia; Larry Jabbonsky, Public Relations Department, Pepsi-Cola Company, Somers, New York; Joan Johnson, Circa Research & Reference, Seattle, Washington; Rachelle Kanefsky, Raincoast Book Distribution Ltd., Vancouver, B.C., Canada; Brookie Keener, Archives Department, The Coca-Cola Company, Atlanta, Georgia; William P. Kloster, Dr Pepper Bottling Co., Museum & Soda Fountain, Dublin, Texas; Paul C. LaCroix, author of *The Clicquot Club Company*, Franklin, Massachusetts; The Library of Congress, Washington, D. C.; Carl F. Mantegna, Hickory Hills, Illinois; Dora McCabe, group public relations manager, Cadbury Schweppes p.l.c., London, England; Alexandra McKee, The George S. Bolster Collection of the Historical Society of Saratoga Springs, Saratoga Springs, New York; The Museum of Modern Art, New York, New York; National Soft Drink Association, Washington, D. C.; National Museum of American History, Center for Advertising History, Smithsonian Institution, Washington, D. C.; John R. Paul, author of *Soft Drink Bottling*, Springfield, Illinois; Clare and Helen Patterson, Jr., Two Fools Antique Mall, Augusta, Kansas; Amanda Pittaway, The Design Studio, Cadbury Limited, Bournville, Birmingham, England; Frank N. Potter, "The Moxie Man" and author of *The Moxie Mystique*, Paducah, Kentucky; Don and Newly Preziosi, Preziosi Postcards, Mendham, New Jersey; Chris Raab, A & W Restaurants Inc., Livonia, Michigan; Carol Roark, assistant manager, Texas/Dallas History & Archives Division, Dallas Public Library, Dallas, Texas; Royal Crown Company, Inc., Ft. Lauderdale, Florida; Andrea Rud, art and production director, Voyageur Press, Stillwater, Minnesota; Milo Stewart, New York State Historical Association, Cooperstown, New York; Steve Sourapas, Seattle, Washington; Rick Sweeney, Painted Soda Bottles Collectors Association, La Mesa, California; Larry Tarantolo, Root 66 Root Beer and Bottling, Indian Head Park, Illinois; Paul Taylor, editor and publisher, *Route 66* magazine, Williams, Arizona; William B. Tilghman, vice president/technical director, Big Red, Inc., Waco, Texas; Catherine VanEvans, Cadbury Schweppes Inc., Dallas, Texas; Anthony G. van Hayningen, manager, Environmental Affairs, National Office, Canadian Soft Drink Association, Toronto, Ontario; Mildred Walker, curator of collections, Dr Pepper Museum and Free Enterprise Institute, Waco, Texas; Jeff Walters, Memory Lane Publishing and author of *Classic Soda Machines*, Camino, California; A. F. Weaver, author of *Time Was in Mineral Wells*, Mineral Wells, Texas; Keith D. Wunderlich, Drayton Plains, Michigan; Ellen Zimny, consumer affairs specialist, The Coca-Cola Company, Atlanta, Georgia.

Michael Karl Witzel
Gyvel Young-Witzel

From Miracle Medicine to Pop Culture

"Soda pop," "soft drink," "limonade," and "carbonated beverage" are all just different names for the same thing: a water-based drink that's artificially charged with bubbles of carbonation and flavored with natural and/or artificial ingredients. Contained within a can, a glass bottle, or dispensed from a fountain mixer, these "pleasure drinks" have replaced water as the number one drink in the United States—and it is fast becoming the premier drink throughout much of the rest of the world. According to a

recent CNN news report, American consumers guzzled a staggering 4.3 billion gallons of soda pop in 1996 alone.

Unlike alcoholic beverages, soft drinks may be consumed in a variety of situations by a diversity of people— young, old, and everyone in between. At work, soda pop offers those who toil a momentary respite and a chance to recharge their thinking. Consumed in automobiles, they provide motorists a welcome form of refreshment and the stimulation to stay alert. On the family dinner table, flavored soda drinks complement the food and clear the palate. At the local cinema, a cold pop washes down popcorn and unsticks Ju-Ju Beans from our teeth.

Dad, Junior, and Seven-Up, 1958
Facing page: During those long-ago crew-cut days of summer, nothing could quench your thirst quite like a cold Seven-Up. *Author's Collection*

**Coca-Cola bathing
beauty trolley sign, 1912**
Right: The first Coca-Cola bathing beauty made her debut in advertising images in 1912. Her "haute couture" bathing costume included long black stockings and beach shoes. *Courtesy of The Coca-Cola Company*

Without carbonated drinks, no picnic, concert, sporting event, or outdoor festival is complete. As the Dr Pepper Company trumpeted in 1923, bottled beverages are "Good For Life!" More appropriately, they're part of it.

There's no denying that soda pop is still gulped down for the sheer enjoyment of the taste. It provides a pleasurable way for consumers to enliven taste buds and achieve momentary serendipity. Naturally, the bubbly characteristics of the formula play a big role: Effervescence clears the palate, invigorates the mouth, and gets the attitude in gear. By their nature, overactive bubbles conjure up images of energy and excitement. Because many of these drinks are laden with carbohydrates, caffeine, and invert sugars (these days, fructose), a quick energy boost is a tangible benefit.

Despite soda pop's ubiquity and niche as cultural icon, its history and development is little known or appreciated. American consumers take for granted the painstaking progress that gave birth to an industry, the slow perfection of product, and the major advancements that make it possible to enjoy refreshing beverages today. Little thought is given to the pioneering inventors, innovative chemists, and industrious manufacturers who first pumped forth the enjoyable waters. Few accolades are reserved for the visionaries who mixed formulas, crafted bottles, and designed the machines to fill them.

And so, this is the reason for this book. Here is the story of that fizzy drink we sometimes refer to as soda pop: how it began, how it developed, and how it poured its way into the popular culture of the United States and then flooded out to satiate the rest of the globe. Within these pages, you will learn about the many triumphs and disappointments of the soda water trade. The progress from home brew to the commercial laboratory, the creativity of the flavor makers, the magic of bottle design, the arrival of new flavors from the fountains, and the many standards that emerged along the way are all distilled into one tasty gulp. *Soda Pop!* will take you on a fun- and flavor-filled journey of discovery.

Pull open the refrigerator or drop some coins into the nearest soda machine and grab a can of your favorite carbonated refreshment. Sit back, pop the top, and take part in an activity that has been going on in one form of another since the late 1700s: quaffing bubbling waters. During the late 1920s, the association known as the American Bottlers of Carbonated Beverages summed it up succinctly: "Bottled Carbonated Beverages—These taste tempting drinks are also known by less formal names . . . tonics in New England . . . soda water in Dixie . . . soda pop in the Midwest . . . soft drinks in the Far West . . . and we all know the ginger ales. Call them what you will, but drink your fill—they're good and good for you!"

Michael Karl Witzel
Gyvel Young-Witzel
Wichita, Kansas
August 1997

Facing page: An array of paper bottle labels from the golden age of soda pop. *Author*

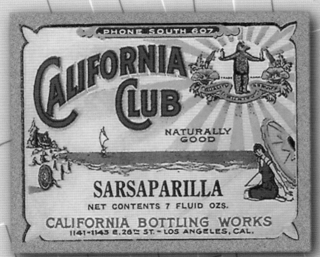

Chapter 1

Forefathers of Fizz

She wieldeth her wand and a potent sway,
Distilling, with magical alchemy
These healing waters. . . .
The Song of the Fountain

With the onset of the nineteenth century, a strange new malaise spread throughout the United States. Referred to as neurasthenia, or total exhaustion of the nervous system, this peculiar affliction of the mind was attributed to the growing complexity of modern civilization. Changing moral values, extended working hours, and cultural stress were all blamed as causes.

Schweppes Royal Table Waters, circa 1900
Facing page: On March 31, 1836, J. Schweppe & Company was honored with a formal Warrant of Appointment as manufacturers of soda water to Their Royal Highnesses, the Duchess of Kent and the Princess Victoria. When Princess Victoria came to the throne in 1837, a new Royal Warrant of Appointment was granted to the firm as purveyors of soda water to Her Majesty the Queen. Since then, successive English monarchs have continued to honor the company with Royal Warrants. This water nymph was painted by Maynard Brown. *Courtesy of Cadbury Schweppes p.l.c.*

"The Champagne of Table Waters," 1910
Right: Perrier, the sparkling French import in the chubby green bottle made its appearance on the American scene in 1907. The mineral water craze subsided but Perrier stayed on, a cultural holdover from the golden era of waters. *Warshaw Collection of the Smithsonian Institution*

In the 1840s, the clinical term *neurasthenia americana* was coined to identify the disease, and before long, frequent accounts appeared in the medical literature of the day. Ill-equipped to deal with the spreading malady, physicians became increasingly alarmed at the flood of patients complaining of stress-related ailments.

Prime candidates for this disorder were the emerging professionals—so-called "brain workers" who toiled in thought-intensive fields like business, journalism, law, and other competitive occupations. These high-strung paper pushers bemoaned a panoply of symptoms, including persistent insomnia, despondency, anxiety, fatigue, debility, and a variety of bodily aches and pains.

"Nature's Remedy," circa 1900
Drilled in 1872, the waters of the Arondack Spring of Saratoga, New York, were heralded as the "ideal table water" to aid digestion. This miracle water acted as an "antidote for all the harmful gases of the stomach" and was "Nature's Remedy for the Stomach, Kidneys and Nerves." Furthermore, as this ad promised, "a glass in the morning fits you for the day's duties, and at night insures perfect rest." *Author's Collection*

In the years following the American Civil War, spread of the infirmity escalated, and doctors increased their attention. New York City neurologist George M. Beard rose to prominence as an expert on the condition and became known as "Mr. Nerves." With aspirations to capitalize on the mysterious malady, the good doctor agreed that the primary instigator of the pandemic was modern civilization and blamed five key factors: steam power, the periodical press, the telegraph, the sciences, and the mental activity of women. The public was starved for quick answers to a complex problem, and Dr. Beard gathered a loyal following of believers.

Mr. Nerves was not alone. Healers of every persuasion took advantage of the growing climate of fear. An ailment that defied rational explanation and exhibited a broad range of ambiguous symptoms was just what they needed to promote their mixed bag of remedies, questionable cure-alls, and restorative tonics—and to rake in the cash. Soon, braggadocio advertisements touting the benefits of previously unknown medical products—from "chloride of gold" to electrical currents—appeared in periodicals. With little restraint—and under no government mandate to tell the truth—the printed missives made the same fantastic claim: By utilizing this unorthodox device or consuming that potion, enfeebled citizens could be freed from stress and nervous disease. At long last, neurasthenia americana had myriad affordable cures. Or did it?

As the hucksters of patent medicines refined the art of marketing useless palliatives, the public's attention focused on the healthful properties of mineral water. In Europe, "taking the cure" at natural springs was long a recognized part of regaining one's health. And, since the water supply in the war-ravaged regions of the American South and the overcrowded industrial cities of the North were often of questionable purity, Americans were ripe for an untainted supply that was bottled at the source. People by the thousands began to swallow countless gallons of mineral water for its curative powers.

Spurred by the overwhelming demand for mineral water, the proprietors of America's mineral springs began distributing advertising materials boasting of unbelievable tales. After major newspapers began printing fantastic accounts of miraculous cures, the river of devotees that consumed mineral water suddenly raged into a torrent. By 1906, people from all walks of life were consuming the natural liquids that bubbled up from the 589 mineral springs in the United States. As dramatic cases of recovery came to light, individual springs gained fame for their unique and astounding healing properties.

One miraculous cure occurred during the early 1900s and was highly publicized. A prominent New York attorney suffering from severe kidney and lower back pains—grave symptoms of disease that had not responded to the usual treatment of bloodletting—was sent by his physician as a last resort to Schooley's Mountain Springs in New Jersey. Here, he began a simple treatment of daily drinking fifteen to twenty glasses of the spring's chalybeate water (a mineral water containing salts of iron). He also embarked on a regimen of light exercise and was administered a special chalybeate mixture that was carbonated. Much to the delight of his physician, the mineral water treatment blackened the patient's urine and within weeks he was deemed "cured."

Those seeking a cure were not required to leave their homes to take advantage of America's mineral springs. Revered by Mohawks as the "Medicine Waters of the Great Spirit," Saratoga Springs's water from New York was some of the first to be distributed in bottles. As early as 1823, the precious liquid drawn from the numerous Saratoga Springs appeared on the market under brand names such as Vichy, Star, Selzer, High Rock, Lincoln, Chief, Victoria, and Carlsbad. By 1900, consumer demand was so great that the Saratoga Springs reserves dropped to a dangerously low level, causing New York to enact laws limiting consumption.

With more healings gaining notoriety, the forefathers of fizz grabbed the spotlight from the makers of pills and potions and gained solid recognition for their belief that water could cure disease. With a theory that was decades ahead of its time, mineral water advocates espoused the belief that trace minerals were essential for all of the body's needs and that consumption of specific minerals could cure specific ailments. As modern chemistry developed, many of these unproved assumptions were found to be true, and the act of pouring healing waters gained new respectability.

Simulating the Effervescent Magic

Although mineral water grew in popularity in North America and Europe, the natural chemical processes that imbued it with bubbles remained a mystery. Lacking empirical data to explain the fizz, mineral water fanciers attributed its magical characteristics to the *spiritus mineralis* (the spirit of the mineral waters) or *spiritus sylvetris* (the wild spirit of the waters).

The first to identify the mineral water vapors as a unique gas was Flemish chemist Jan Baptista Van Helmont in 1620. It wasn't until 1782 that French chemist Antoine Laurent Lavoisier determined that the gas was carbon dioxide.

Experiments directed at duplicating the animated characteristics of mineral water began long before there was any understanding of its chemical properties. The first documented attempt to simulate the bubbling water occurred when Swiss alchemist Thurneysser produced a small amount of artificial mineral water in 1560. In 1732, Dutch physician Hermann Boerhaave made a key step toward creation of artificial carbonation when he extracted gas from chalk, calling the substance *acidum vagum fodinerum*. In 1767, Englishman Richard Bewley produced the first mixture that combined bicarbonate with carbonated soda water (fossil alkali), dubbing the new concoction a Mephitic Julep.

At the same time, Briton Dr. Joseph Priestley embarked on related experiments with "fixed air." His investigations began at the local brewery where he tried

Vichy water, 1893
One of the world's most famous spa areas is the Vichy hot mineral springs of France, where the thermal waters are promoted as a restorative for those with liver and stomach disorders. For those unable to afford the trip to France there is an alternative: a bottle of Vichy water exported directly from the source. To promote this bottled export, the Vichy Company gave out free samples and souvenir pamphlets at the World's Columbian Exposition of Chicago in 1893. *Author's Collection*

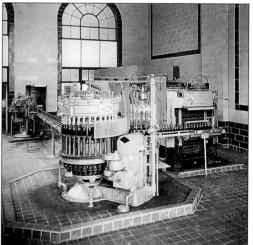

Saratoga Spa bottling plant, 1937

Left: Bottling machines were revolutionized during the 1930s. The Meyer Dumore Filcrowner used here by the Saratoga Spa Park Bottling Plant in 1937 was a combination rotary filler and crowner developed in 1931 by the George J. Meyer Mfg. Company of Cudahay, Wisconsin. Ten larger-capacity Meyer machines were installed in 1938 at the Pepsi-Cola plant, Long Island City, New York, each with a capacity of two hundred bottles per minute. *George S. Bolster Collection of the Historical Society of Saratoga Springs*

Saratoga Vichy home delivery, circa 1940s

Above: In 1872, the Saratoga Vichy Spring was drilled in Geyser Park, in the resort area of Saratoga Springs, New York. To everyone's awe, the spring's chemical composition resembled the famous Vichy Spring of France and contained a higher bicarbonate of soda and lower salt content than any of the other Saratoga Springs. Home delivery of Saratoga Vichy Water was established by the 1890s. After the turn of the century, the gas engine replaced horse power, but the Saratoga Vichy Spring Company chose to retain the time-honored tradition of wagon delivery. *George S. Bolster Collection of the Historical Society of Saratoga Springs*

Drinking pavilion at Saratoga Springs, 1875

Above: The Mohawk Indians discovered the naturally carbonated waters of Saratoga Springs, New York. They considered the waters a health-giving gift of the god Manitou and kept its location a guarded secret. This tranquil state of affairs ended in 1758; after a lengthy land dispute, the springs were turned over to settlers. Still, the location of the springs remained secret until they were officially discovered in 1770. By the 1850s, the swampy wilderness was transformed into a bustling resort with luxury hotels, genteel amusements, and fancy drinking pavilions. By 1875, crowds of guests gathered to drink the healing waters. *Frank Leslie's Illustrated*, August 7, 1875

High Rock Spring and dipper boy, circa 1880

Above: Layers of insoluble carbonate deposits formed the unique volcano-like mound of High Rock Spring; this phenomena also produces the strange shapes known as stalagmites and stalactites. Glasses at the end of long-handled dippers were plunged into the spring by dipper boys who served the eager crowd. The bubbling waters were free, but the dipper boys worked for tips. *George S. Bolster Collection of the Historical Society of Saratoga Springs*

Interior of Congress Spring Pavilion, circa 1880

In 1880, the rolling grounds of Congress Spring Park at Saratoga Springs contained lush gardens, lively fountains, and meandering paths dotted with inviting benches. Bandstand music serenaded promenaders while they enjoyed the scenery. Across the lawn stood the magnificent Congress Hall Hotel and the stained-glass splendor of the Congress Spring Pavilion, complete with water bar. During the early 1800s, the temperance society made its presence known: Visitors could not drink anything stronger than the waters and orchestras played only hymns; anything as "unseemly" as dancing was prohibited, and gambling and other vices were not tolerated. But it was hard to keep the pleasure-loving resort goers down: Within a few years, the morality issue was overturned, and visitors once again returned to dance, gamble, and drink liquids more powerful than the spring waters.
George S. Bolster Collection of the Historical Society of Saratoga Springs

to duplicate natural carbonation by combining fixed air with water. He was later able to use sulfuric acid to liberate gas from chalk and "impregnate" water, as he termed it, with the gas after a vigorous shaking.

Although Priestley was not the first to experiment with carbonating apparatus, his conclusions were unique. Priestley first observed that atmospheric air must be removed from the carbonation process. He also recognized the importance of using a pump to saturate the water with greater quantities of carbon dioxide by compressing the gas and completing the final process of absorption with pressurized agitation. All of these clever deductions would become a vital part of commercially carbonated water, earning him the distinction as father of the industry.

Priestley's pioneering carbonation system was refined in 1774 when Dr. John Mervin Nooth appeared before the Royal Society of London to present a brand new device for producing carbonated water. This apparatus combined all the features of Priestley's into one convenient unit. Because of its practical utility, the Nooth carbonating device became the first major step in the evolution of commercial carbonation equipment.

As the equipment for making soda water improved, advancements in related technologies finally allowed scientists to make a reliable chemical analysis of prominent European spa waters. The most popular waters that were used by apothecaries and physicians to treat digestive problems, rheumatism, and gout were found to contain alkaline salts. Other aperient, or purgative, waters boasted the salts of iron, lithium, and even barium. More potent mineral waters were found to be fortified with high amounts of sulfur and arsenic.

With the basic makeup of mineral water deciphered and practical carbonation equipment available, the ability to bring these bubbling potions to the general public at an affordable cost was made a reality. Mineral-salt powders were easily obtained in bulk from chemical supply houses and could be mixed with ordinary water in any number of different combinations and concentrations. The water was then artificially aerated with a carbonating system.

In 1764, Thomas Henry set up the first commercial operation to make carbonated water for public consumption. Henry opened an apothecary shop in Manchester, England, and set in motion an industry that would one day spread around the globe. As a recognized treatment for fever, scurvy, dysentery, bilious vomiting, and other stomach disorders, the centerpiece of his fledgling beverage outlet was none other than Bewley's Mephitic Julep. As did its inventor, Henry advised imbibers that the tonic should be taken with a "draught of lemonade" or a mixture of vinegar and water. These ingredients would cover any offensive taste and supposedly release the much-touted fixed air in the stomach. Before long, the enterprising Henry modified Nooth's carbonating device with the addition of a large cask, allowing him to produce greater quantities of carbonated water more efficiently.

There were more advances to come. The ongoing quest to perfect a commercial method for creating soda water was aided in 1789 when Frenchman Lavoisier debuted a new invention called the gasometer. A unique gadget that consisted of a large wooden cylinder bound with strong iron hoops, the gasometer collected the gas generated in a separate vessel; the gas was then pumped into the water. This device—when combined with the carbonation principles established by Priestley and the productivity of the Nooth device improved upon by Henry—formed the foundation for the coming age of commercial carbonation machines.

Enter the Man Named Schweppe

With artificial mineral water now readily available, consumers soon came to desire the freedom of buying soda water at outlets that were more convenient and readily accessible than a spa or even the local druggist. If soda water was to attain a greater level of practicality, personal, portable containers—and the methods to fill them—were called for. This basic need of the market became the impetus for the field of bottling.

While there were many individual inventors that contributed to this commercial sphere before the turn of the century, no entrepreneur is regarded with more romance than Jacob Schweppe. Schweppe established himself as England's—and the world's—first commercial bottler and manufacturer of artificially made seltzer and spa waters. With his involvement in several businesses for producing these healing waters, he uncapped a chain of events that would one day affect the entire industry of carbonated beverages and the standardized methods used to package drink.

Schweppe was born into a German farming family in 1740. Although his parents probably hoped for a strapping lad to assist with the physical labors of their agrarian lifestyle, their offspring grew to be a delicate tike. Ironically, it was this physical deficiency that allowed young Jacob to shake off a life otherwise destined for hard labor and choose for himself a less strenuous occupation.

At the age of eleven or twelve, a wide-eyed Jacob bid goodbye to his parents and apprenticed with a traveling tinker. He soon became a silversmith and graduated to jewelry making before emigrating to Switzerland. In 1777, he achieved the highest distinction in his professional guild when he was recognized as a *maitre-bijoutier*.

Having attained respect and financial distinction, Schweppe found time to pursue outside interests. He regarded himself as an amateur scientist, inspired by Lavoisier and Priestley. After reviewing Priestley's seminal pamphlet "Directions for Impregnating Water With Fixed Air" of 1772, he became enchanted with creating carbonated water.

Schweppe conducted a few of his own experiments and was so determined to find the answers that he abandoned all of his other occupations in order to succeed. Like many of the scientists who tested the bubbling waters before him, his goal was to produce carbonated liquids in grand quantities.

Amazingly, his unschooled dabbling in the craft of conjuring up carbonic gas yielded him a substantial amount of quality mineral water. Schweppe was then surprised to find that there was a demand among Geneva citizens for a fresh supply of the tonic. With that, his experimentation turned into commercial development.

Although organizing a firm to make

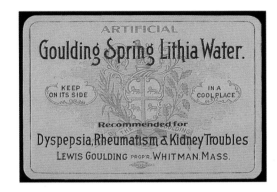

Goulding Spring trade card, circa 1800s
Mineral water makers were vigorous promoters of the miraculous health benefits of their wares. Natural and artificial waters like Goulding Spring Lithia Water were endorsed as cure-alls for myriad ailments. For decades, the mineral water hype continued unchecked—until the 1890s, when the U.S. government stepped in. By this time, the medicinal benefits of mineral water were criticized by the American Medical Association. Then, in March 1898, a National Pure Food and Drug Congress was organized to fight food adulteration and false advertising. One of its investigations was the fraudulent claims made by mineral water makers. By 1906, the Pure Food and Drug Act was passed, and the end of the mineral water craze officially arrived. *Warshaw Collection of the Smithsonian Institution*

Pluto Water stamp, circa 1850s
The town of French Lick, Indiana, was founded in 1811 and named for a nearby salt lick and French trading post. When a local physician tapped into the commercial potential of the area's three artesian springs, the town grew into a resort. By the 1850s, French Lick became a popular destination for health seekers, and Pluto Spring a popular brand. The spring is still open to the public today, but visitors must bring their own containers. *Warshaw Collection of the Smithsonian Institution*

carbonated water was foreign to him, Schweppe saw there was great room for improvement. He constructed a unique and practical line of carbonating machinery from the ground up. Crude by today's standards, this set of apparatus (later known as the "Geneva" system) was characterized by a mixing enclosure with an internal agitator. This "generator" created carbon dioxide gas by forcing sulfuric acid up through two barrels of chalk dust. The carbonic gas that bubbled up was fed by tubing into a gasometer, the large, inverted storage tank suspended aloft by counterweights. This immense cylinder was open on the bottom where it was mated with a wooden carbonating vessel that was bound with strong iron hoops. After it passed through purification vessels, filtered water was fed into this tank. When the gasometer filled up with carbonic gas, the counterweights were released, and it dropped into the water vessel. The resulting pressure of the freed tank caused the gas to be dissolved into the water as a hand-cranked compression pump supplied additional pressure.

Schweppe now possessed the ability to aerate water to equal—or exceed—the aeration of natural mineral waters. At the same time, he could produce enough mineral water to make a commercial business viable. Solving these problems, Jacob Schweppe assumed his rightful place as the founder of the soft drink industry in 1783.

Over the next ten years, Schweppe established himself in Switzerland and sold mineral water far and wide. Due to the rapid expansion, he hired a trusted friend whose name has been lost to history and transferred sales duties to him. As part

of his job, the gentleman was allowed free reign of the factory and the carbonating machine. That was a mistake.

The man betrayed the friendship, deciding to go into business for himself. He approached well-known engineer Nicholas Paul to build a duplicate of the Schweppe apparatus. When the machine was complete, he planned to terminate the relationship, take company secrets with him, and set himself in direct competition with Schweppe.

In the end, the business plan failed as the gentleman fell victim to a double cross himself: Paul held back his best concepts and engineered an inferior facsimile of the Schweppe setup while at the same time producing an improved version for himself. Although the minerals added were invisible and the waters transparent, more than one person saw the gold that could be extracted from the carbonated waters.

To avoid a heated battle, Schweppe extended an olive branch to Paul in the form of a partnership. Formed in 1790, this new alliance included Paul's father, Jacques, a skilled mechanic and inventor. But Nicholas Paul was still not satisfied. As soon as the agreement was formalized, he convinced his longtime friend and advisor, Henry Albert Gosse, to join them in business, as Gosse was a well-known Geneva pharmacist who had also experimented with mineral waters.

A few months later, the foursome organized as a partnership called Schweppe, Paul and Gosse. In September 1790, the *Journal de Geneve* officially announced the partnership's intent to make duplicates of "famous spa waters for the enjoyment and physical benefit of consumers." Finally, the elements were in place to pour out sparkling seltzers all over Europe.

A Good Drink Is Finally Recognized in England

Schweppe's reputation was soon put to the test. The partners decided that it was time to enlarge the business and establish a factory in England. Choosing a partner to perform this task was difficult: Because of his father's illness, Paul did not want to leave Geneva, and Gosse had his pharmaceutical outfit to run. By default, the task fell upon Schweppe.

Schweppe came to London in January 1792, and upon arrival, his aspirations were dashed: Along the cobblestone streets, horse-drawn wagons laden down with crocks of mineral water were everywhere, delivering to local apothecary shops and hospitals. A few enterprising vendors were even selling flagons of fresh mineral water on the street to passersby.

Despite the competitive climate, Schweppe established a modest factory on Drury Lane to begin production in the spring. He installed the manufacturing equipment, including an improved version of his carbonating apparatus with a pressure gauge.

The partners believed the key to success in England was through product endorsement by physicians. But Schweppe was dismayed to discover that there was little interest even with referrals. It appeared that the public didn't have any desire to try a product without a reputation or name.

Finally, Schweppe received recognition, the praise coming from noted philosopher and writer Erasmus Darwin, Charles Darwin's grandfather. Erasmus Darwin heard of Schweppe's water

in 1794 from industrialist Matthew Boulton, who wrote to him, "Mr. J. Schweppe, preparer of Mineral Waters, is the person whom you have heard me speak of and who impregnates it so highly with fixable air as to exceed in appearance Champaign and all other Bottled Liquors." Boulton elaborated on the three different strengths of the Schweppe's water, noting that each of the concentrations had its own significant health benefit, depending upon the quantity of alkali it contained. The first concentration was for drinking with dinner, the second for nephritic patients, and the third reserved to treat only the "most violent" cases.

In February 1793, France declared war on England just as the Schweppes partners went to war with each other. The partnership was in jeopardy, but as continental travel was halted, Schweppe could not return to Geneva. In 1796, the partnership was broken: Gosse and Paul received equal shares of the Geneva firm, while Schweppe maintained exclusive rights to the London operation. Within months of the dissolution, Gosse and Paul also split. Meanwhile, Jacob Schweppe prospered.

Bottling the Bubbling Elixir

Jacob Schweppe was the first to commercially bottle mineral water, and there is evidence that he also introduced the first bottle designed specifically for carbonated water. In 1789, a year before his ill-fated business journey to England, he was given a sketch of a "bottle" or jar to take with him. Part of the partner's plan was to produce this portable container in stoneware.

This particular bottle was to be pro-

Foxhunter Spring Water, 1911
Advertisements in *Town and Country* magazine had snob appeal in mind, featuring products of unquestionable taste where price was rarely an object. This June 1911 issue featured cool New York summer getaways and, of course, Foxhunter Spring Water. *Warshaw Collection of the Smithsonian Institution*

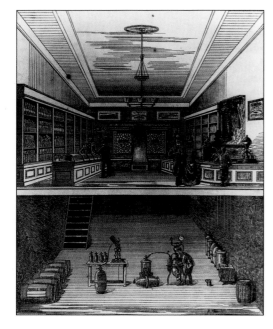

Creating soda water, Tufts catalog, 1885
In 1863, James W. Tufts needed a soda fountain for use in his Somerville, Massachusetts, drugstore but found the available choices lacking. As a result, he designed a unique fountain he called the Arctic with a series of metal coolers that produced extremely cold soda water and eliminated the need for shaved ice, which dissipated the carbonic gas. The invention's popularity led him to sell his drugstore and enter the fountain business. His 1885 fountain equipment catalog provides a glimpse into a fledgling industry: "The object of this engraving is that persons not familiar with soda-water apparatus may understand what is necessary for the manufacture and dispensing of soda-water." *Collection of The New-York Historical Society*

duced in an ovoid shape with a small, flattened area as its base, allowing it to stand on end when necessary. To seal the container, a cork was placed into the neck, secured with a string, and then tarred over. A label imprinted with the product name and signature of one partner as a quality seal was affixed over the stopper. On the shoulders of the bottle were two handles or "lugs" that dovetailed with the distinctive egg-shaped design.

The earliest documented use of the egg-shaped bottle (without a flat feature found at the base) was around 1809, and it was used concurrently by both Jacob Schweppe and William Hamilton, the inventor of the "continuous system" of carbonation, who described a similar container in his 1809 patent application for his machine. Even though the earliest examples of the Schweppe stoneware or glass bottles were imprinted with his London bottling plant's address at 79 Margaret Street (dating them between 1809–1831), it's not certain whether Schweppe modified the sketch into the simplified ovoid bottle or not. He never patented the idea.

The ovoid configuration performed a specific purpose and did it well. The rounded end forced those handling the bottles to keep them on their side during transport and storage. This kept the cork moist at all times to ensure a proper seal, a high priority since insuring the integrity of the seal was necessary to stop the precious carbonic gas from escaping. Because the bottle couldn't stand upright and toppled over without the assistance of a holding jig, the style was known as the "drunken" bottle.

There was one more reason for using the egg-shaped bottle: In harmony with the day's methods for manufacturing glass bottles, the design lent itself admirably to a uniform thickness of glass when it was being blown. This attribute was significant to the bottlers doing business before 1900, since any weaknesses or flaws in the pressurized container increased the possibility that the bottle might burst.

When compared to the svelte soda packaging used today, the drunken bottle used by the early Schweppe's dynasty—and his competitors—appears to be a cumbersome and impractical container. Though undeniably homely, it was nonetheless the best bottle that time and technology could offer and was so perfectly adapted for the industry that it remained the standard for more than a hundred years. Until fast and efficient modern methods for manufacturing bottles of clear, sculpted glass came along, these peculiar ovoid bottles that caused customers to refer to the drinks they contained as "egg sodas" would remain the state of the art.

America Bottles the Magic Bubbles
The fame of Schweppe and his mineral waters spread to North America and piqued the interest of many would-be

Schweppes bottles assortment
Facing page: Among the numerous shapes, sizes, and configuration of bottles that were once used by J. Schweppe & Company, the clay and green glass egg-shape bottles (pictured in the foreground) are the most famous. These crude containers used in the early days of soda bottling date from 1809. Note that while the company was named after Jacob Schweppe, it typically referred to its products as "Schweppes." *Courtesy of Cadbury Schweppes p.l.c.*

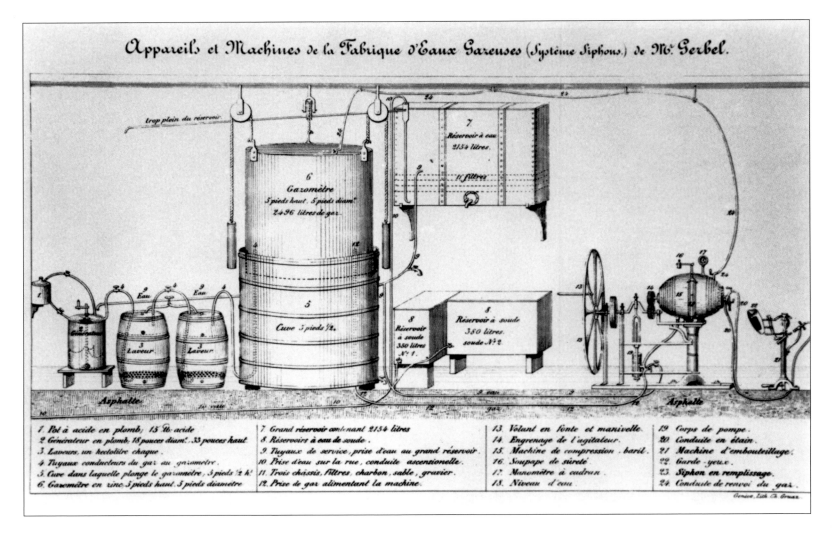

Appareils et Machines de la Fabrique d'Eaux Gazeuses (Système Siphons.) de Mr. Gerbel.

1. Pot à acide en plomb, 15 ℔ acide	*7. Grand réservoir contenant 2134 litres*
2. Générateur en plomb, 18 pouces diam!. 33 pouces haut.	*8. Réservoirs à eau de soude.*
3. Laveurs, un hectolitre chaque.	*9. Tuyaux de service, prise d'eau au grand réservoir.*
4. Tuyaux conducteurs du gaz au gazomètre.	*10. Prise d'eau sur la rue, conduite ascensionelle.*
5. Cuve dans laquelle plonge le gazomètre, 3 pieds ½ h!	*11. Trois châssis, filtres, charbon, sable, gravier.*
6. Gazomètre en zinc 5 pieds haut. 5 pieds diamètre	*12. Prise de gaz alimentant la machine.*

13. Volant en fonte et manivelle.	*19. Corps de pompe.*
14. Engrenage de l'agitateur.	*20. Conduite en étain.*
15. Machine de compression. baril.	*21. Machine d'embouteillage.*
16. Soupape de sûreté.	*22. Garde-yeux.*
17. Manomètre à cadran.	*23. Siphon en remplissage.*
18. Niveau d'eau	*24. Conduite de renvoi du gaz.*

Genève, Lith. Ch. Gruaz.

"Geneva System" of carbonation

The principals of the semi-continuous Geneva system were developed by Jacob Schweppe circa 1780. This system consisted of a carbon dioxide generator, gasometer, and pump that forced the carbon gas into a carbonating chamber, where it mixed with the liquid. When the liquid was thoroughly impregnated with the carbon gas, it was drawn off, and the operation was repeated again. *Courtesy of Cadbury Schweppes p.l.c.*

imitators. Baltimore, Maryland, resident Joseph Hawkins was one of the curious. During the early 1800s, Hawkins crafted an improved version of Schweppe's carbonating apparatus, but with one key difference: This one was patented in the United States in 1809—the first legal record of the nation's growing interest in mineral waters.

Two years before the patent was issued, Hawkins journeyed by carriage to the progressive city of Philadelphia, Pennsylvania, to scout out a promising location for what many historians agree

was the first U.S. artificial mineral water manufacturing operation. The former capital and busy port town was an excellent choice as it teemed with commerce and offered entrepreneurs a fertile market to cultivate.

In 1807, Hawkins joined with partner Abraham Cohen, and the waters commenced to flow. It didn't take long for the pair to receive accolades in publications of the day, including the *Register of the Arts* for May 1808: "Mr. Joseph Hawkins, who introduced the manufacturing of these waters into Philadelphia, has made a very important improvement in the process. The mineral water by machinery of his contrivance, and for which he has obtained letters patent from the government of the United States, is raised from the fountain or reservoir in which it is prepared under ground, through perpendicular wooden columns, which enclose metallick tubes, and by turning a cock at the top of the columns, the water may be drawn without the necessity of bottling. The reservoir being placed under ground, and frigid preparations occasionally made use of, the mineral water is rendered more cool, refreshing and grateful to the taste."

Despite the promise of success, Cohen eventually withdrew from the association. Hawkins continued and soon acquired another collaborator by the name of Shaw. From a soda fountain housed in an establishment known as Shaw and Hawkins, they served fizzing flagons of mineral water at Philadelphia's 98 Chestnut Street. Prices were fair for the time, as a dozen corked bottles of the soda waters known as Pyrmont or Ballston were priced from one to two dollars depending on size.

While the bottles were made available to home users or to exporters who were planning to ship them overseas, Hawkins instituted other promotions to move his mineral waters out the door: Instead of selling a glassful for the standard six cents, monthly subscriptions were sold for the bargain price of $1.50. Subscribers were entitled to consume one glass of the precious refreshment a day, and the discount became popular with the regulars. With a positive cash flow, the future of Shaw, Hawkins, and mineral water was secure.

At the same time, Benjamin Silliman was collecting his own converts to the carbonated drink in New Haven, Connecticut. His involvement with the business began in 1805, shortly after being appointed head of Yale University's new chemistry department. As part of his research into the miracle of carbonic gas, he went to Europe to gain firsthand manufacturing knowledge. During the time he spent in London, Silliman was impressed by Schweppe's commercial bottling methods. When he returned to the United States in 1807, Silliman opened a bottling plant of his own to market high-quality mineral waters exclusively to upscale New York City businesses.

Silliman used his knowledge of chemistry to advantage. Unfortunately, his experience in the realm of mixology didn't carry over to bottling. No sooner had he started than a disturbing problem threatened to shut him down: His pressurized containers were exploding.

At the time, a pottery house in New Haven crafted Silliman's bottles, and it was obvious they had little expertise in the art of constructing structurally sound containers. Most of the flasks delivered to Silliman burst, and much of the carbonated product was wasted. It was an embarrassing situation: Bottles often self-destructed at the most inappropriate times, frightening bystanders and causing retail vendors to question the product's stability.

Desperate to save the business, Silliman hastily abandoned the idea of using crockery bottles to hold his mineral waters and began looking for alternatives. He remembered that the English bottlers had mastered the art of

Schweppes delivery wagons, late 1800s
Clunky steam wagons were used to deliver Schweppes waters during the transition from horse-drawn wagons to gasoline-powered vehicles. During the late 1800s, the English Thornycroft Steam Wagon Company, Ltd., manufactured these new workhorses for a wide market. *Courtesy of Cadbury Schweppes p.l.c.*

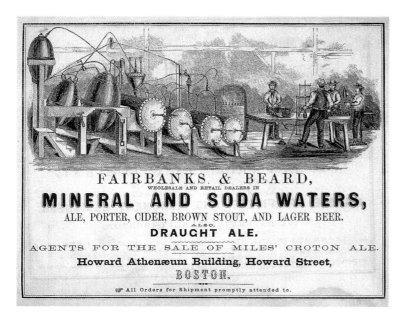

Fairbanks & Beard ad, 1858
Diversification was the key to success for the early bottler. This typical bottling plant of the mid-1800s added mineral and soda waters to its product list. The foot-operated bottling table (shown at right) had just emerged, supplanting the labor-intensive methods of the "knee bottler." *Warshaw Collection of the Smithsonian Institution*

making containers, and without delay, he arranged to buy discarded British soda water bottles. He purchased foreign containers secondhand, cleaned them, filled them with his own sparkling water, and rebranded them with his own label.

Silliman's method saved the day and became an early example of the now politically correct practice of recycling. Of further significance, it signaled the onset of an industry trend in the field of American soda bottling: a foreshadowing of the returnable, reusable, refillable, resealable, cash-deposit bottle that would rise to ubiquity during the coming centuries of carbonation.

Owens Builds an Automatic Bottler

While Silliman's solution was bold, not everyone could utilize recycling as a solution for their bottling woes since discarded imports were in short supply. Most contemporaries entering the business were forced to seek out existing bottle makers in America, which was also a problem as the supply of domestic containers was minimal. Up until 1892, most of the American-made bottles were hand-blown and -finished. The process was tedious, skill driven, and labor intensive.

Glassblowers had a virtual lock on the market, even though their time-honored techniques were laborious and slow: First, the trained artisan dipped a "pontil," or hollow steel tube, into a hot crucible of molten glass. The pontil was revolved rapidly, and by way of centrifugal force, a "gob" of glass formed on the end. The glassblower removed the dipstick and blew air through the tube into the gob until it formed a bubble. With care and skill, this molten bubble of glass was placed onto a stone slab where, still attached to the pontil, it was worked into a suitable shape for a mold.

The amorphous hunk of glass was placed into an iron mold made of two parts connected by hinges. After the mold was closed, more air was blown into the glass until it gradually assumed the bottle shape of the mold. When the glass cooled, it was removed from the form and the pontil snapped off. The final touches called for the lip and neck to be finished by hand in order to remove sharp edges. Using this precarious method, a glass blower and four assistants could produce about two hundred bottles in a fourteen-hour day. If the industry of carbonated beverages was to prosper, someone would have to find a better way.

That someone was Michael Owens. During the late 1890s, he was employed by the Toledo Glass Company in Ohio and learned firsthand of the difficulties involved in bottle manufacturing. In 1895, he began experimenting with a mechanized bottle maker. With the introduction of his first semi-automatic unit, Owens made strides toward streamlining the process. By 1900, he constructed a completely automatic machine that received a U.S. patent in 1904.

The automatic Owens bottling machine signaled a revolution. Central to its design and overall function was a circular, rotating framework. This moving

Schweppes Soda Water, circa 1900
The term "soda water" was coined to describe the addition of soda (or alkali) to artificially carbonated water. Originally, this beverage was consumed for a variety of medicinal purposes, and its specific "soda" properties were distinguished from ordinary mineral water in ads of the age. The first record of the "soda water" designation dates back to a 1798 essay written by Neapolitan Dr. Tiberius Cavallo in England in which he describes Schweppes soda water. That same year, soda water was named in a Schweppes advertisement. Artist Maynard Brown painted this Schweppes wood nymph.
Courtesy of Cadbury Schweppes p.l.c.

Nichols mineral water fountain, 1858
During the 1850s, mineral water dispensers were still relatively simple affairs. This Nichols countertop device of 1858 featured two draft arms and a hollow center cylinder. This circular cavity contained a coil of pipe that led directly to the draft arms. The druggist packed the cylinder with ice, cooling the soda water as it flowed into a glass held below. *Author's Collection*

assembly supported a number of working bottling units, each outfitted with a bottle-blowing mechanism and mold. When these units were immersed into a revolving pot of molten glass, the necessary gob was captured and blown into the mold. The entire process was completely automatic and, in one broad stroke, changed the bottling industry.

For the first time in the history of the carbonated beverage, bottles—in virtually any configuration—could be produced with unequaled economy in quantity and quality. Within a few years, the Owens machine took the industry to new heights, and by 1917, two hundred Owens machines were at work. Finally, national expansion and distribution were within the realm of possibility.

The Growing Demand for Bottles

As the demand for bottled drinks that could be swigged at home, consumed in a carriage, or taken on trips increased, soda fountain operators realized that the ever-increasing number of bottlers were taking away their business. To win back market share, many decided to start up seasonal bottling operations in their own back rooms. And why not? During the late 1890s, before the onset of regulations and red tape, it was easy. For $3,000, almost anyone could break into the bottling biz.

One of the newfangled bottling tables was the most important element in the process, such as the popular foot-powered models from the Hutchinson Company. Approximately the size of a modern dining room table, it was akin to a work bench where all the elements—water, bottles, flavorings, and corks—came together. With it, one could single-handedly fill and seal bottles of drink.

At the same time, full-scale bottling factories that housed rows of heavy-duty bottling machinery could whip up copious quantities of charged water and package it in a short amount of time. By 1875, professional bottlers were experimenting with advanced methods of producing carbonic gas and found their answer in the Bramah system, a method favored by the industry after mid-century.

Named after British inventor Joseph Bramah (the man responsible for early designs of the hydraulic press) this method was similar to the processes used by the individual operator. It consisted of a larger version of the usual gas generator, a gasometer, force pump, and a carbonating vessel containing pressurized water and gas. There was one big difference: Because water and carbonic gas were constantly fed into the production loop, the carbonating process was never interrupted. Among the cognoscenti, it was termed the "continuous system."

As the advent of the continuous system spawned the creation of innovative gadgetry to automate the bottling process even further, Dr. W. Raydt of Germany began making waves in the bottling pond in 1886. To everyone's great amazement, Raydt changed the course of mineral water manufacturing when he found a way to manufacture "liquid" carbonic gas. With great optimism, Raydt trapped the gas in metal cylinders and began exporting the substance. At first, North American bottlers had problems adapting to the supply, and it failed to catch on.

Meanwhile, similar advances were being made in the United States. Within two years, Philadelphia College of Pharmacy graduate Jacob Baur began marketing his own liquid carbonic gas, and it was soon hailed as the undisputed way of the future. It was 1888 when Baur's Liquid Carbonic Acid Manufacturing Company shipped out its first cylinder of compressed gas to an American customer. Soon, a spate of competitors followed suit, and the race to reap the financial benefits of the new substance was on.

It was soon obvious that the liquid form held distinct advantages over the older methods and proved to be a boon to the entire industry. It allowed the bottler to produce higher quality carbonated water and, at the same time, simplified the number of manufacturing steps. As an added bonus, bulky carbonating machines and raw materials were no longer necessary, and more resources could be allocated to sales and promotion. Thanks to these innovations, the bottled beverage industry entered an era of rapid growth, and soon the virtues of carbonated water were known to virtually every man, woman, and child in North America and Europe.

The Gadgets That Topped It Off

As the methods of making bottles and filling them with carbonated drink were perfected, there was one area that remained in a constant state of flux: the bottle stopper. By 1892, more than 1,500 patents were registered in the United States alone for various types of soda bottle closures. Because containers varied in size and shape, there was no universal answer when it came to sealing them up.

For this reason, most bottlers of the era stuck with the 2,000-year-old method of using small, round plugs made from the bark of the cork oak tree. For the small-scale soda water manufacturer, corks were easy to incorporate into the production line. To stop up bottles, one operator with a strong arm required only a pair of tongs, a few twists of wire, some foil, and a good, heavy mallet. After they were soaked in hot water, natural corks could easily be coaxed into the necks of soda bottles with minimal effort.

Despite this inherent utility of the cork, there was one aspect of its use that caused problems. To save a few dollars, a few unscrupulous bottlers chose to bypass the suppliers in Spain and Portugal and simply purchased used, unsanitary corks (by the bucket load) on the open market. Like those that collect aluminum cans today, down-and-out citizens of the late 1800s gathered discarded corks for resale. Because a vast majority of these "found" corks were at one time used in champagne bottles (containing alcohol), newly bottled soda water often became contaminated with a strange bouquet.

Shrinkage of the stopper was a serious problem too, since the porous wood material takes up less space when the water it contains evaporates. Invariably, this was one of the main reasons that early bottles leaked so much, lost their pressure, and began seeping carbonated liquid. This factor constrained the first bottle designs to the round-bottom motif; while positioned on its side, the liquid inside of a bottle remained in constant contact with the cork and helped it to perform its job. However, if the bottle was turned on end for too long, the stopper would eventually dry out and begin to deteriorate under pressure. Finally, the fizz would go flat.

The problems inherent with the com-

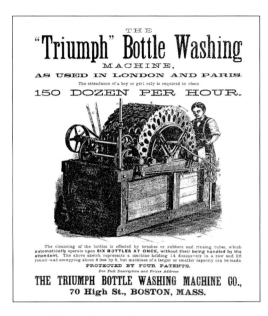

Triumph bottle washer, 1886
The Triumph Bottle Washing Machine Company, of Boston, Massachusetts, advertised its Triumph bottle washer in 1886. The drum's side pockets held six bottles for a total capacity of 150. The one-hour cleaning cycle required to prepare bottles for reuse included soaking, brushing, and rinsing. *Courtesy of John R. Paul*

mon cork forced inventors to come up with a new bottle stopper. In 1865, John Matthews, Jr., patented a clever "gravitational stopper" in the United States. As an internal stopper that was self-contained within the bottle, his idea consisted of an elongated plug that poked through the neck and was connected to a small, metal stopper. This sealing element was fixed into place by the pull of a strong magnet. When the plug (kept in place by strong carbonation) was pushed in, the pressure seal was broken and the entire stopping device fell into the bottom of the bottle. Unfortunately, everyday customers didn't have an electromagnet at their disposal, so resealing was a problem.

Eight years later, British inventor Hiram Codd patented a gizmo he called the Codd Ball Stopper. Equally effective as the gravitational stopper, his design featured a hard rubber or metal "sealing ball" that was to be packaged inside of the bottle. After the soda water container was filled with the carbonated beverage, it was inverted, causing the heavy ball to settle against a gasket positioned in the neck. Once the ball was in place, the internal pressure held the stopper tight—even after it was turned upright.

To open the Codd stopper, consumers required a narrow object that could be thrust into the neck to dislodge the ball from the sealing ring. The ball then fell down to the bottom of the bottle and remained there as refreshment was poured. Of course, the sinking behavior of the stopper was a big disadvantage if the entire contents weren't consumed in one sitting; it too could not be resealed. While it never gained a loyal audience in North America, it gained wide acceptance in overseas markets.

In the United States, a variation of the European stopper became quite popular. Known as the "floating ball stopper," this practical variation was popularized by many bottling suppliers, particularly by S. Twitchell and Brothers of Philadelphia. Made of metal or rubber, their ball stoppers were hollow and floated on the liquid after being popped. During the filling process, bottlers didn't have to turn the bottle upside down—eliminating yet another step in the process.

However, none of these stoppers came to dominate the industry as did the internal stopper made by the W. H. Hutchinson Company of Chicago. Patented in 1879, its unique seal was amazingly simple, utilizing a rubber disk attached to a bent "spring" stem. Bottles fitted with the Hutchinson were easily opened by pushing down on the wire and forcing the disk out. The spring's shape interacted with a special contour inside of the bottle neck that limited the stopper's vertical travel so it didn't drop in. At any time, the consumer could pull up on the wire hook, shake the bottle, and reseal it—preserving the carbonation for future occasions.

Because bottlers could reuse over and over again the bottles that were outfitted with the Hutchinson stopper, it proved to be an economical route. Within a few years, most competing brands of bottling tables were refitted with special Hutchinson attachments. The cork became a vestige of the past.

In short order, a raft of Hutchinson imitators began to flood the market with similar stoppers. A melee of one-upmanship soon followed and was

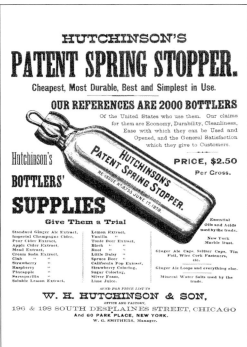

Hutchinson spring stopper advertisement, 1886

Far left: A plethora of internal stoppers flooded the market by the late 1800s, but one rose to dominate the field: the simple and economical design patented by Charles G. Hutchinson of Chicago on April 8, 1879. The clever design permitted the bottle to be opened by pushing the stem into the bottle neck while the wire loop prevented the stem from falling back into the bottle. The reverse operation pulled up the rubber disk, closing the bottle. *Courtesy of John R. Paul*

Johnson Crown Bottle Cap Machine, circa 1910

Left: William Painter's small metal cap with cork liner and ribbed skirt revolutionized bottling. The Baltimore, Maryland, resident began work on the new closure in 1889. The original cap featured an exaggerated, long skirt with deeply crimped depressions. To aid in its removal, a loop was attached to it (this was before the invention of the bottle opener and twist-off cap). This gave it the appearance of a miniature "crown," a term so appropriate that it became generic. Improved versions were developed in 1890 and 1891. On February 2, 1892, patents were issued to Painter for all three versions, followed immediately by Painter's new capping machine. On April 1, 1892, the Crown Cork & Seal Company was organized, capitalized at $1 million. Crown Cork & Seal is still in operation today. *Courtesy of the Dr Pepper Museum, Waco, Texas*

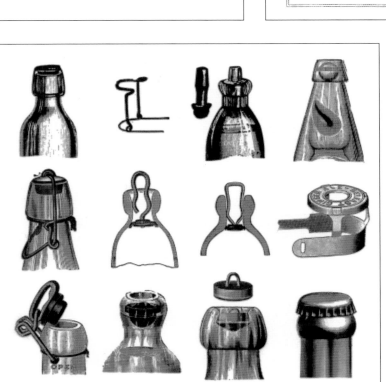

Early bottler stoppers

Left: Predecessors of the crown closure, top row left to right: cork; cork fastener of 1857; Matthews gravitating stopper of 1865; Codd Ball Stopper of 1873. Center row left to right: Lightning stopper of 1875; Hutchinson stopper of 1879; Klee stopper of 1880; Bernadin bottle cap of 1885. Bottom row left to right: Joly stopper of 1885; Twitchell floating ball stopper of 1885; bottle seal of 1885; crown cap of 1892. *Reprinted with permission, National Soft Drink Association*

fought out in the trade magazines as patent infringement lawsuits were filed by all parties. Amos Parkhurst was the main litigator, claiming he invented the first internal bottle stopper in 1878—registered long before the Hutchinson.

Nevertheless, the bottle stopper battles were forgotten almost as fast as the cork. In 1892, William Painter, a man regarded as Maryland's most prolific inventor, debuted a radical bottle stopper called the "crown cork," which first saw full-scale production when the Crown Cork & Seal Company began cranking out endless barrels of them later that year. Unfortunately, the initial reception was rather chilly.

Dubious of the new format, beer brewers and soda water makers did not believe that a tiny metal cap lined with a thin cushion of cork could keep their products from spoiling, exploding, or leaking. To them, Painter's brainchild looked like a clever sham.

Luckily for the industry, they were wrong. Painter won the affections of North American bottlers when he staged a dramatic demonstration of the crown cap's sealing properties. For the test, a large brewery capped a cargo of beer with the new crowns and sent it on a round-trip South American journey. When the test shipment returned, all of the bottles were secure. No flaw could be found in the caps or the brew despite the heat, roll of the ship, and rough handling.

For the first time in the history of beverage, a sanitary, single-use sealing method was available for forward-thinking bottlers. By 1895, the process was even more streamlined: That year, Painter unveiled the first multiple-head, rotary-crown capping machine with an automatic cap feed. At long last, the assembly line had come to bottling.

The crown cork seal was christened the king of bottled beverages, and within a few years, it became the standard around the globe. Crown Cork & Seal Company flourished, and by 1928, the international sales from its bottling equipment totaled $11 million. Today, Painter's simple idea to crimp a metal cap on a bottle has grown into a multinational company with an income in excess of $109 million.

All early stoppers made a "pop" sound when they were opened, which was no doubt the impetus for the term "soda pop." But to this day—steadfast against the continuing onslaught of twist-off caps, pull-top lids, and other such extravagances—the bottle cap remains a favorite for all those who like to feel the coolness of glass in their hand and the jerk of a bottle opener when they snap off the cap. In the end, that sudden, dramatic rush of carbonation escaping from the uncapped bottle is what soda pop is all about.

"The cork is branded" ad, circa 1930s
As demand for bottled waters grew, so did the need for good cork stoppers. This created an inflated price for new stoppers and disreputable people began re-selling used corks. Champagne corks were in high demand as they could be cleaned, recut, and inserted into another bottle. Sixty cents bought a pail of used champagne corks; thirty-five cents a bucket of corks from other beverages. These prices were highly motivating as a diligent worker could easily double his normal income. This unsanitary practice created a stir in the periodicals and stern warnings to consumers and bottlers. To reassure the public, Schweppes began using branded corks. Cork makers stamped the company's name directly into the cork during production. Since the Schweppe name was imprinted on the cork, it discouraged reuse by others. Although the crown cap eventually replaced the cork, the practice of labeling the bottle with the words "see also that the cork is branded" remained, a visible reminder of another era. *Courtesy of Cadbury Schweppes p.l.c.*

33

Crazy Water

THIS IS THE HOME OF CRAZY WATER

CRAZY WATER HOTEL, MINERAL WELLS, TEXAS — "WHERE AMERICA DRINKS ITS WAY TO HEALTH"

Crazy Water Hotel, 1929
Above, top: Mineral Wells, once the playground of the rich and famous during the 1920s, is now a quiet Texas town. Gone are the movie stars, the big bands, and the crowds. But remnants of the past remain. Today, the Crazy Water Hotel still stands—a thriving and peaceful retirement residence. *Courtesy of A. F. Weaver*

Crazy Water Crystals
Above, bottom: While the rest of the world was sunk in the Great Depression, the Collins brothers were making a fortune on green-and-white packages of Crazy Water Crystals. No longer would the sick and frail have to travel to Texas to receive the cure—it was now available in a box. Purchasers had only to add their own water and drink. *Courtesy of A. F. Weaver*

Today, the remnants of a once-booming mineral water business can still be seen in the town of Mineral Wells, Texas. Originally built as a seven-story luxury resort, the Crazy Hotel is now a retirement home, the Milling Sanitarium a VFW hall, and the towering Baker Hotel—once the playground of screen stars, crooners, and oil tycoons—sits empty, a silent reminder of the times when the healing waters flowed.

When James Lynch arrived on this site in 1877, there was little indication that this area would one day become a magnet for visitors. Although the valley was beautiful and the soil productive, well digging wouldn't release water from the earth. Stuck with eighty acres, the Lynch clan was forced to haul water from the Brazos River. After three hard years, a traveling well driller arrived in town and struck a deal to sink a hole. To everyone's chagrin, the dig unearthed a foul-smelling liquid.

Necessity forced the family to overcome their aversion to the water, and one by one they drank. After feeling no ill effects, they deemed it safe. Weeks later, something strange happened: Mrs. Lynch's rheumatism had vanished! After word of the cure spread, throngs of health seekers arrived at the farm. When the hundreds turned to thousands, Lynch drilled more wells and then built a town.

Eventually, the stampede caught the attention of speculators, including a colorful character known as Uncle Billy Wiggins. He purchased his own parcel of land and proceeded to cash in on the medicinal waters. According to town lore, a woman who was convalescing at the local sanitarium spent her days under the shade trees surrounding the well, sipping its effluent nectar. Resident juveniles nicknamed her the "crazy woman" and after she left town cured of mental distress, the curative spring assumed the "Crazy Well" name. Wiggins took advan-

tage of the incident and added a pavilion and bottling plant.

In 1907, Sidney Webb purchased the Crazy Water Company from Wiggins, along with the four other wells. He went on to erect the town's first luxury hotel, appointing it with modern bathrooms, elevators, telephones, and convenient access to the ever-popular pavilion.

Inside the pavilion stood an elaborate bar that boasted four different strengths of Crazy Water. After filling up with drink, visitors exercised on the "Fat Man's Reducer": one thousand wooden steps winding up East Mountain. From a vantage point below, locals made a sport of spotting novices: The poor souls who dared ascend the stairs after over-indulging in Crazy Water often turned an about-face to beat a hasty retreat to the nearest toilet.

Tragedy struck in 1925 when the hotel and entire downtown block were consumed by fire. One year later, Dallas businessmen Carr and Hal Collins resurrected the Crazy to the tune of $1 million. Ironically, the seven-story beauty they constructed prompted the locals to take aim at out-of-town investors. Determined to wrestle back control of their water rights, local citizens formed a committee to clear the way for an even more elaborate structure. Aided by reputable hotel magnate T. B. Baker, the new Baker Hotel would boast fourteen stories and four hundred rooms.

Suddenly, the competition for tourists became an all-out war. To counter their lavish competitor, the proprietors of the Crazy Hotel installed a giant "Welcome to Mineral Wells, Home of Crazy" sign at each traffic access to town. On the rooftop, a gargantuan electric billboard flashed the Crazy name far and wide. Inebriated by the battle, many of the local shop owners incorporated the word into their names. By the end of the twenties, a plethora of "Crazy" businesses appeared, including the Crazy Laun-

> *"There is considerable excitement in the county below the mountains beyond the river concerning a well that has been dug, the waters of which seem to be benefiting those who drink it."*—J. H. Baker, July 21, 1880

dry, Crazy Drugstore, Crazy Theater, Crazy Drugstore, and Crazy Beauty Shop.

After the stock market crash of 1929, Carr embarked on a campaign to market the snowy white powder that remained after Crazy water evaporated. Hal Collins extolled the virtues of Crazy Water Crystals on *One Man's Opinion,* a live radio show broadcast from the Crazy Hotel. A wry mix of humor, country wisdom, music, and product testimonials, the show stirred up sales of $3 million a year.

Unfortunately, principals at the Food and Drug Administration were listening in too. Suddenly, all unwarranted health claims had to be removed from radio spots and packaging. The Collins brothers complied, removing the bromide that claimed the crystalline powder was useful in the treatment of "rheumatism, functional stomach diseases, cystitis, diabetes, and Bright's disease."

One year later, Crazy Water Crystals made a surprise appearance at Chicago's Century of Progress Exposition. Hal Collins attended and was drawn to a prominent display entitled the "Chamber of Horrors." Here, all of the medicinal cures that resulted in blindness, hair loss, and even death were on display. To his surprise, a green-and-white box of Crazy Water Crystals was neatly tucked in among the profane. To make matters worse, photos showed the Mineral Wells hotel and bottling plant.

Collins was aghast at what he saw and immediately had the Crazy Water Crystals removed from the exhibit. Unfortunately, the damage was already done. Sometime later, the company was forced to add a warning label that read: "Not to be used when abdominal pain (stomach-ache, cramps, colic), nausea, vomiting, or other symptoms of appendicitis are present. Continual use of any laxative may develop a systemic dependence on same." Crazy Water was on its way out.

Despite the controversy that surfaced over the crystals' efficacy, Collins never wavered in his loyalty. When he sold the hotel and mineral water rights in 1947, he reserved a large cache of the crystals for himself. Every day for the next thirty-three years, he religiously consumed his daily dose. He passed away at the respectable age of eighty-seven, a valid example of the healthful benefits of Crazy Water.

Nevertheless, his final testimony went unrecognized. By the fifties, the heyday of healing waters in America had concluded. Most of the grand temples erected to celebrate the curative powers of mineral water had closed their doors and ceased operating. By 1958, the animated electric sign that once welcomed the throngs to Mineral Wells and the home of Crazy Water was torn down. Sold for scrap, it spent the last of its days among the rubble of a Dallas junkyard.

Hal Collins and the Crazy Gang, circa 1930s
The homespun wisdom of Hal Collins, the knee-slapping hijinx of his entertainers, and songs from the Crazy Gang band provided the perfect promotion for Crazy Water Crystals on the radio airwaves. Collins's lively variety show was broadcast directly from the lobby of the Crazy Hotel in Mineral Wells. During the show, it wasn't unusual for enthusiastic audience members to extol the virtues of the crystals. The popularity of the show eclipsed all expectations, and in June 1932, it was broadcast nationally by the NBC radio network. Crazy Water Crystals were known coast to coast! *Courtesy of Gene Fowler*

Chapter 2

Flavorful Fantasies

The flavor manufacturer is interested in separating or duplicating and compounding the odorous substances of natural ingredients in order to create the various sensations which are called flavor.
Joseph Merory, *Food Flavorings: Composition, Manufacture, and Use,* 1960

Collins Pharmacy, Islip, Long Island, circa 1900
Facing page: During the early days of the 1900s, retail establishments like the Collins Pharmacy in Islip, Long Island, provided a wide range of goods and services to the public. Along with the sales of film, box cameras, postcards, matches, tobacco, liquor, and other patent medicines, enterprising druggists of the day peddled myriad carbonated creations. Dressed in crisp, white uniforms, the soda jerk (at right) and pharmacist (center) were the keys to a smooth-running operation. *Library of Congress*

King of Beverages, poster, circa 1906
Right: Between 1889 and 1890, Dr Pepper co-founder Wade Morrison and Waco, Texas, bottler R. S. Lazenby created a brand new Dr Pepper trademark. The company's first slogan, "King of Beverages," was paired with the colorful image of a majestic lion. The first ad to use the format was painted on a prominent Waco building by artist Louis Sternkorb. For years, the stately animal hawked the product, implying that "Vim, Vigor, & Vitality" could be had just by downing a bottle of the sweet, flavorful beverage. *Courtesy of the Dr Pepper Museum, Waco, Texas*

During the summer of 1870, a new attraction caught the fancy of the bustling Wall Street financial district. While temperatures rose, thirsty crowds flocked to Delatour's refreshing soda water stand. Specializing in the sale of bubbling waters, Delatour's offered ice cold drinks during the peak hours of business. In a city plagued by sizzling hot summer days, the frigid temperature of his drink was a major draw—resulting in long lines of eager customers all clamoring for a taste.

Delatour's process was unique: By placing several portable fountains inside an ice-house and refrigerating them overnight, he could produce a beverage that was not only cold but also highly carbonated. The next day, the chilled fountains were transferred to large metal tubs, packed in ice, and hurriedly transported to the Wall Street storefront. There, they remained submerged in ice while a goose-neck spigot allowed the refreshment to flow. Once the liquid was drawn into a glass, customers could pick from an extraordinary selection of chilled syrups and have them mixed with the water. An infinite variety of

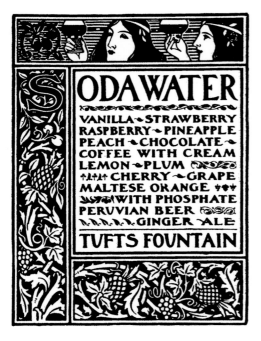

Tufts Fountain poster, 1890
At retail soda fountains, displays such as this Tufts poster informed customers of the flavors and proprietary brands available. During the fledgling days of soda pop, carbonated drinks were mixed up directly at the fountain: One dispenser yielded the carbonated water, another the flavoring syrup; the two were combined by the fountain operator and served. *Courtesy of John R. Paul.*

flavored sodas could be blended on the spot, and as a result, Delatour's tiny storefront soda stand gained a faithful following.

Although the excitement for Delatour's chilled flavorful fantasies was certainly new, his soda fountain was not. Developed decades earlier in response to the apothecary's demand for a countertop soda water dispenser, the first fountain was patented by Samuel Fahnstock of Lancaster, Pennsylvania, in 1819. Fahnstock's probably wasn't the first countertop dispenser, but he was the first with the foresight to give it the name "fountain." Equally important, the design of Fahnstock's dispenser was unique, since it featured an earthenware lining that inhibited the metallic contamination of the carbonated water, an unwanted taste often caused by copper-clad tin liners.

Splendor of the Soda Fountains

Since the pharmacist administered and prescribed soda water to his clients, countertop dispensers quickly became a necessary fixture in an apothecary. But there were soon problems: Eager patrons began sipping up such a copious amount of mineral water that the equipment became outmoded. New fountains with the capacity to satisfy the increasing crowds were needed.

Fortunately, there were inventors and manufacturers who were ready to enter the infant field of soda fountain equipment. Each contributed at least one important element to the technology of soda water dispensing.

The so-called "Neptune of the Trade" was John Matthews, Sr., who earned the honorary title in an 1868 issue of the New York *Evening Mail*. He started in the bot-

tling industry in 1832 and introduced the commercial soda water trade to the United States. His son, John Matthews, Jr., later followed in his footsteps to become a prolific inventor of both bottling and fountain equipment.

Another early innovator was Gustavus Dows, a former druggist from Lowell, Massachusetts. He became the first to use his imagination in giving the dowdy fountain a makeover. In 1861, he ushered in a new era of drugstore elegance by introducing North America to the first soda fountain made of polished marble. His patented marble box contained a cooling coil, metal containers to hold the flavor syrup, and an ice shaver; ornate, silver-plated syrup faucets enhanced his distinctive fountain.

Also in 1861, Boston's Alvin D. Puffer debuted his "Magic" draft tube. Whereas old designs required a separate tube for each flavor, Puffer's clever arrangement allowed numerous syrups to be drawn from a single faucet. After a particular flavor was drawn from the tube, an operator moved a lever and disconnected the mechanism from the syrup source. At the same time, it was reconnected to the carbonated water. When the water rushed through on its way to the drinking glass, any syrup residue left in the dispensing tube was flushed out, leaving it clean for the next customer's flavor selection.

In 1893, James W. Tufts abandoned his lucrative drugstore in Somerville, Massachusetts, and entered the choppy waters of the fountain trade to invent and patent an apparatus styled the "Arctic." Although a crude machine by modern standards, it was revolutionary at the time. It featured cylindrical metal coolers that produced soda water so cold that shaved ice, which destroyed carbonation, was no longer needed. The syrup containers were placed in the rear of the marble box and connected with the faucets by coolers passing beneath the ice, producing chilled syrups.

After the success of his Arctic fountain, Tufts opened his own successful soda fountain manufacturing firm in Boston. By 1864, Tufts's first catalog was mailed to soda fountain proprietors, and each successive catalog featured an increasing array of elaborate designs. But the best was yet to come.

In 1876, Tufts teamed up with Charles Lippincott to obtain the exclusive rights to the soda-fountain concession and advertising at the Philadelphia Centennial Exposition. Over thirty feet (9 meters) tall, the exhibit featured three stories of opulent splendor: soda water dispensers and syrups were located on the ground floor; the second story featured fountains of perfumed waters; and the top floor an elegant crystal chandelier. Finishing touches included a jungle of rare exotic plants, ferns, and flowers. With its dazzling silver-plated filigree, ornate statues, and colorful glass globes, the towering display attracted crowds of onlookers, and by the exhibition's end, the fountain area had served up thousands of ice-cold, flavored sodas to the thirsty. Gone forever were the days of the homely, cottage-style fountain. In the decades to come, soda fountains were destined to increase in size and majestic splendor.

Early Additives Were Viewed as Medicine

A power far beyond just industry publicity events soon arose to promote the wholesome appeal of the soda fountain. By 1873, membership in a group called the Woman's Christian Temperance Union was growing. Led by Francis Willard, the organization became a powerful force in the United States by encouraging its female membership to protect the "sanctity of the home and family." Their method for dealing with drunkenness? Hoards of women swooped into those pits of decadence known as saloons and shamed the patrons into leaving.

Although American women didn't yet have the vote, they managed to upset the alcoholic apple cart in most of the major cities. In 1888, the group achieved victory when the Republican party quietly included the subjects of "purity of the home" and "temperance and morality" in their political platform. Soon thereafter, the bar keepers began losing business as family-oriented soda fountains opened their doors. In large cities, restaurants such as New York's Tontine Coffee House began serving effervescent fare. A few gutsy saloon keepers even started offering carbonated water.

About that same time, a handful of adventurous souls were experimenting with the art of creating soda water flavorings. Ironically, it was the same practices that were born of the distilled spirits trade that aided them in their quest to develop palatable formulas. After all, it was the early North American settlers who imported beer-making skills from their native Europe to produce the first "non-alcoholic" beers. During those times, beverages were made for the whole family to enjoy.

Not only did the addition of birch, spruce, sarsaparilla, ginger, and other flavorings effectively disguise the taste of inferior drinking water, it also created a pleasing treat for the family. Like their counterparts made from grain, family-

The Commonwealth.

The Commonwealth, A. D. Puffer & Sons Manufacturing Company, 1889
Manufactured in Boston, Massachusetts, the Commonwealth soda fountain was sold through the A. D. Puffer & Sons catalog at the height of the soda fountain's golden age. The three spigots dispensed regular and carbonated water; beneath, a row of smaller valves released an assortment of syrup flavorings into the serving glasses. At first, these grandiose units were called "fountains," but the term later became more generalized, and by the Roaring Twenties, it described the counter area where sodas and ice cream were served. *Collection of The New-York Historical Society*

"Makes You Younger," circa 1910
Ads from the Uncle Sam Company of Atlanta, Georgia, typified the outlandish claims that were made by many drink and patent medicine makers emerging before the 1900s. Not only did Uncle Sam "Freshen and Brighten the Intellect," it "Tickles the Palate" and "Satisfies the Thirst." More important to most drinkers, it was the drink that "Makes You Younger!" *Courtesy of John R. Paul*

style beers were produced from honey, sugar, or molasses and fermented with yeast. With an alcohol content of up to four percent, the resulting beverage was slightly carbonated and easy to swallow. So popular were these home brews that by 1857, *Beecher's Receipt Book* of home recipes included a formula for ginger beer, which called for the addition of bicarbonate of soda to enliven the recipe.

Disguising the taste of inferior drinking water to create a taste treat was only a secondary use for ginger flavoring. At the time, health benefits were much more important, and the consumption of ginger ale was viewed as highly therapeutic. And why shouldn't it? With its medicinal qualities, dried ginger root first gained a foothold as a precious spice imported from the Orient and even today is listed as a beneficial drug in the *Chinese Pharmacopoeia*.

Recognized for its calming effects on the digestive system and its ability to inhibit vomiting, ginger ale was a bottled beverage that already had an established following in Europe. It was only natural that North Americans would love its sweet and snappy flavor too. Imported brands of ale like those bottled by Cantrell & Cochrane of Ireland were prized by people who could afford them. Thus, it was no surprise when Lemon's Superior Sparkling Ginger Ale became the first soft drink trademark to be registered in the United States, in 1871.

Ginger wasn't the only additive put on a pedestal for its healing qualities. The curious sarsaparilla root was equally adored as an ingredient for health. As early as the sixth century, it was widely used as a remedy for venereal disease (with minimal results) and was also re-vered for its beneficial effects on the digestive system. When combined with the extracts of other "medicinal" plants, it was often employed to treat rheumatism, gout, pulmonary, and cutaneous (skin) diseases.

After highly vocal physicians like Dr. J. C. Ayer of Lowell, Massachusetts, touted sarsaparilla as a blood purifier, the root gained a public following that bordered on outright mania. With little scientific evidence to back it up, the medical claims for sarsaparilla multiplied as consumers embraced any and all products that contained it. At many of the nation's soda fountains, it became the favorite flavoring. The demand was so overwhelming that by 1871, sales of various sarsaparilla remedies (and other products) made Ayer one of the wealthiest men in America.

Despite the fact that the sarsaparilla root actually contained few if any medicinal properties, the American population held firm in its faith for the root. The continuing frenzy for sarsaparilla elicited this apologetic statement in the 1879 National Dispensatory: "Although Sarsaparilla has been proven to be almost inert as a medicine, its name is familiar to the people as a blood purifier and they have faith in its curative virtues." Regardless of its effectiveness, it remained a much-admired additive for sodas.

Housewives Rave for Root Beer

For the North American homemaker who was already burdened with an ample supply of housework, mixing up batches of root beer, ginger ale, or sarsaparilla mead was a time-consuming and often thankless chore. Fortunately, a solution was at hand. While honeymooning in

Coca-Cola ad, 1904

Above, left: By 1900, many saloon keepers bowed under the pressures of the temperance-minded Anti-Saloon League of America and closed their doors. Others removed all evidence of previous liquor affiliation and reopened as soda fountains. By 1916, twenty-one states had banned saloons and the soda fountain business boomed. For the first time in history, men, women, and children could enter the new fountain parlors, walk up to the bar, and order refreshing beverages together. *Courtesy of The Coca-Cola Company*

Circle A ginger ale bottles

Above, right: Named for his cattle brand, Circle A Ginger Ale was introduced by R. S. Lazenby of Waco, Texas, in 1884. Like all good ginger ales, this one was aged—for four years—in sealed wooden casks. In 1885, Lazenby and Wade Morrison formed the Artesian Manufacturing & Bottling Company, which made both Circle A and Dr Pepper. Although the sparkle and snap of Circle A Ginger Ale gained a loyal following, by 1922 increased competition cut the market share of the Texas ginger ale, and it was finally retired in 1940. The company—by then named the Dr Pepper Company and based in Dallas—concentrated its full attention on Dr Pepper. *Courtesy of the Dr Pepper Museum, Waco, Texas*

Dr. Brown's Sarsaparilla bottle label, circa 1910

Left: During the 1800s, sarsaparilla's popularity as a "blood purifier" spilled over into the production of home root beer. Within a few decades, sarsaparilla syrup was concocted by druggists and served at the drugstore fountain. By 1922, however, it was difficult to find a sarsaparilla soda that actually contained any real root. That year, the *Beverage Journal* announced a new standard: A soda flavor labeled as sarsaparilla didn't have to contain any sarsaparilla! Instead, the flavor was defined as one made with oil of sassafras, oil of wintergreen, or oil of sweet birch—with or without sarsaparilla. Dr. Brown's sarsaparilla and cream soda can still be found today. *Warshaw Collection of the Smithsonian Institution*

Hires' trade card, 1892

Above: These miniature billboards advertised extract used by homemakers to mix up batches of root beer at home. Sold in a familiar light brown carton, "Hires' Improved Root Beer!" was really a good deal. For just twenty-five cents, one could craft a personal supply of the bark-and-berry brew at home with a minimum of fuss and bother. *Preziosi Postcards*

Hires' trade card, 1892

Right: Trade cards appeared on the market in the mid-1800s and were one way businesses introduced a service or product. Comprised of card stock, the average size of these promotion vehicles was a scant 3x5 inches (75x125 mm). When the chromolithography process was introduced, the cards bloomed with color, and by the 1900s, trade cards were at the height of their popularity. Among extract makers, Hires' made the greatest amount of cards; "An Uninvited Guest" was a whimsical example. *Preziosi Postcards*

New Jersey, Philadelphia pharmacist Charles E. Hires sampled a great-tasting herb tea made from an unusual mixture of natural ingredients. He was captivated by the flavor and upon returning to his drugstore, began experimenting with roots, berries, and bark to recreate the effect. He called his product Hires' Herb Tea and promptly sold it from his apothecary.

It didn't take long for Hires to realize that his tasty recipe could be effectively used by the homemaker to produce home-brewed root beer. Although she would still have to cook the mixture, strain it, add the right proportions of sugar and yeast, ferment the brew for ten hours, bottle the mixture, and age it for a few days, she could now rest assured that the flavor would be uniformly good, time after time. At last, trial and error was eliminated from the procedure. And, the expensive ingredients required to make root beer would no longer have to be purchased separately.

Not surprisingly, the time- and cost-cutting advantages of Hires's formula propelled the product to local fame. At the 1876 Philadelphia Centennial Exposition, tiny packages of the mixture made their industry debut. Although Hires didn't have his own booth, he still managed to pass out sample packets to exposition visitors. With the seeds for expansion planted, he turned his attention to the root beer business and began a national program of selling directly to the home consumer. The pre-mixed ingredients would also be marketed to druggists and fountains at wholesale cost.

Happily, his evangelism for root beer was a success. In an era when many businesses failed, Hires proved himself a mer-

chandising genius: To hook new customers, he passed out free samples whenever he could. Then, capitalizing on the age-old principle of giving extra value for value received, he added a special bonus in the form of a trading card with each package of his formula. Children and adults alike were smitten by the wit and whimsy of the miniature billboards and began collecting them with enthusiasm. The colorful trading cards became such a popular feature that Hires's sales soared.

Hires still wasn't satisfied. In 1880, he introduced a liquid extract of his famous formula that further reduced the homemaker's workload. Armed with a tiny flavor flask, she was now excused from the tiresome boiling, straining, and skimming that was once required for home brewing. To promote the improved product, ads ran in *Harper's Weekly* and *Harper's Monthly*, but they were hardly needed: Liberated women of all ages gladly showed their devotion by purchasing massive quantities of Hires' Improved Root Beer.

As the temperance movement gained momentum, the Hires brand attained new importance. By then, it was not only considered a delightful drink, but a respectable "temperance beverage" suitable for all ages. Confident in the loyal following, the Crystal Bottling Company began bottling Hires' in 1893. Soon after, the bark-and-berry drink could be purchased by the glass at soda fountains.

Finally, a nation of women were truly liberated from the time-consuming chore of home brewing. With minimum bother, packaged and ready-to-drink bottles of Hires' could be purchased down at the Main Street grocery. With the work hours

Hires' Improved Root Beer ad, 1884
During the uncomplicated age of horse-drawn surreys, the first ad for Hires' Improved Root Beer appeared in *Harper's Weekly* in 1884. Customers were instructed to see their local druggist for a bottle of extract, or order it directly by sending in twenty-five cents by mail. *Reprinted with permission, National Soft Drink Association*

The Pioneer Bottling Works labels, circa 1927

The Pioneer Bottling Works was founded by the Einbeck family, German immigrants who were bottlers of beer and soda in Wisconsin. One of the Einbeck boys moved to Washington state around 1900 and built a bottling plant. He died of typhoid fever in 1917 and left his wife and three children—Arthur, Amanda, and Gertrude—to carry on the business. The last surviving child sold the operation in 1982. *Author's Collection*

that were spared, the American homemaker finally had time to take a break, relax, and really enjoy a foaming, frothy mug of delicious root beer for herself.

Soda Syrups Gain a Fountain Following

Although Hires was among the first to gain widespread recognition for creating an effective home brew extract, the first use of concentrated flavoring syrups was reported in the Philadelphia *Journal of Health* in 1830. According to early recipes, these soda flavorings were produced by simply mashing ripe fruit into a pulp. The resulting mash was then pressed through a fine sieve and the juice collected in a stoneware pan. Sugar and water were added and the viscous liquid poured into bottles. After they were boiled for twenty minutes, the containers were corked and stored on their side in a cool place.

Unfortunately, producing a quality product wasn't as easy as it sounded, since the advent of flavored beverages brought with it a whole new set of problems. One of the most disturbing was the propensity of flavored soda water to turn rancid if it was stored for too long. The essential oils used to make the flavorings contained terpenes and other unstable constituents that often went bad, ruining the drink. Fruit juices had drawbacks as well, since they were rich in fermentable sugar and yeast. A safe, effective way to preserve bottles of flavored soda pop was unknown during this early phase of bottling.

Some of the early bottlers compounded these spoilage problems by adding a foam producer. The rationale was that if a dense "head" could be created

on the beverage after it was poured, carbonation would escape at a slower rate. Unfortunately, these frothing agents were made from a solution of saponin (a glucoside found in some plants), and many critics decried their use as unhygienic. They had good reasons for their suspicions, since the lather-inducing ingredients emitted a foul odor. Even worse, they tasted offensive and made a beverage "ropy." In light of this, some countries outlawed altogether the use of foam producers in bottled soda products.

Still, there were experimenters who dared to extend the limited horizons of the flavoring field. While operating a small Philadelphia perfumery shop, Frenchman Eugene Roussel made a mark by bottling a lemon-flavored soda in 1838.

A decade later, Henry Tilden of the Tilden Company, one of North America's first pharmaceutical houses, made a major contribution to the field when he extracted the concentrated properties from the much-ballyhooed sarsaparilla root in a stable base of alcohol. Although Tilden sought the medicinal aspect of herbs and not their ability to provide flavoring for carbonated waters, it didn't take long for others to recognize the limitless potential of alcohol-based compounds. While featuring a high flavor concentration, these new compounds circumvented the existing problem of ingredient decay. Now, soda pop makers could move beyond the bland format of unflavored mineral waters with complete and unabashed confidence. The essence industry was born, and by 1900, food and drink would be a lot more fun.

The American soda fountain proprietor could choose from a vast variety of

Society Club Raspberry coaster, circa 1910
Above: Manufactured and bottled by the Society Club Beverage Corporation in Newark, New Jersey, Society Club Raspberry was one of many early beverages that were made with natural spring water and fruit extraction. *Warshaw Collection of the Smithsonian Institution*

Schweppes ginger ale, ad circa 1920s
Left: In the early 1800s, ginger beer was already made by several companies, including Schweppes. But the first ginger ale didn't appear until mechanical carbonation was invented. Credit for development of this snappy beverage belongs to Dr. Cantrell of Belfast, Ireland. Between 1849 and 1852, the Cantrell & Cochrane firm shipped ginger beer to British troops in India but the long voyage proved that ginger beer was susceptible to easy spoilage. So, Cantrell set out to find a substitute with better preservation properties. The result was ginger ale, a clear, pleasant-tasting, easy-to-produce beverage. The Irish beverages became popular in North America where they were referred to as Belfast and Dublin ginger ales. Schweppes introduced its own version of dry and sweet ginger ale in the 1870s. Dry ginger ale often contains capsicum (red pepper). *Courtesy of Cadbury Schweppes p.l.c.*

Fighting the "watermelon fiend," circa 1913

Below: During summers in the 1880s, sales of soda pop dropped dramatically, especially in the American South. What was causing the problem? The watermelon! Experts suggested that the "watermelon fiend" was capable of driving an entire soda water plant out of business. To counteract the threat, bottlers experimented with fruit-flavored beverages, including melon. Unfortunately, the attempts failed because of spoilage woes. Salvation arrived in the early 1900s with new fruit extraction equipment and scientific flavoring techniques. At last, Southern bottlers had the arsenal they needed to fight the watermelon threat! By 1913, a new lineup of fruity drinks included a Southern classic: the sweet dark cherry (usually reserved for pies), smashed (pits and all) into Fowler's Cherry Smash. During that same year two other brands appeared: Cherry Blossoms and Cherry Julep. *Preziosi Postcards*

"Three Ways to Get Hires," 1933

Above: During the 1930s, the Charles E. Hires Company embarked on an aggressive marketing campaign to educate the public about cheap imitations. The growing market for root beer had attracted unscrupulous firms who used oil-flavored substitutes and harmful foam producers such as saponin. Hires was quick to point out that his root beer was entirely natural—"like drinking fresh juice"—and made from the extracts of sixteen roots, barks, herbs, and berries all blended in a slow, costly percolating process. And, according to the ads, ninety-six out of one hundred doctors preferred the purity and fine flavor of Hires! *Author's Collection*

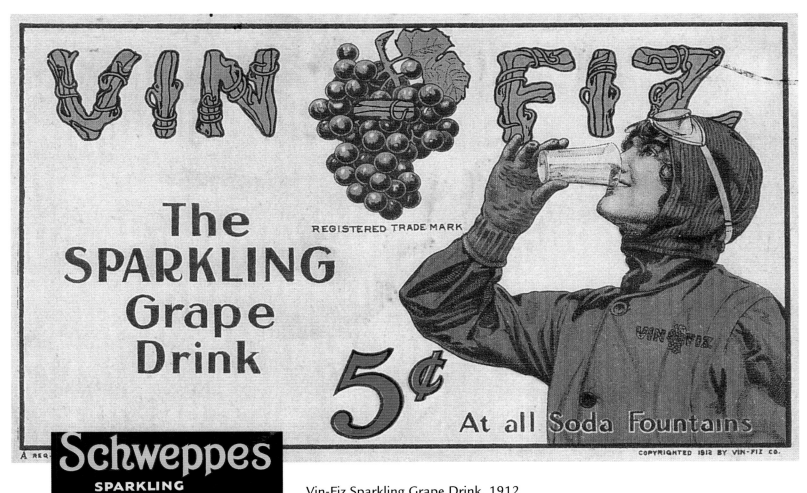

Vin-Fiz Sparkling Grape Drink, 1912

Above: By 1896, there were several new flavors at the fountain, including cherry and orange, but it was still tough to create a realistic grape flavor. Grape syrups originally started with a wine-based extract, usually from a catawba (a red grape) wine. Eventually, the catawba grape lost its popularity to the robust flavor of the dark concord grape. Then, as the making of artificial flavoring improved, bottlers were at long last able to produce a tasty grape beverage. By 1910, the grape flavor was in, and several bottled brands appeared on the market including Grapine, Grape Julep, Grape Mist, and Grape Smack. A cold Vin-Fiz could be purchased in 1912 at the fountain for a nickel. *Preziosi Postcards*

Schweppes Sparkling Lemon ad, circa 1930

Left: Schweppes introduced its first lemon-flavored soda in 1835. The product, named Aerated Lemonade, was a departure from the usual Schweppes soda and artificial mineral water, but lemon-flavored beverages were nothing new—even in 1835. Lemonade was a favorite as far back as the 1600s. In France, itinerant vendors of lemonade dispensed the liquid from tanks strapped to their backs. By 1676, the French government recognized the trade and granted a monopoly to the "Campagnie de Limonadiers." Although carbonation was added in the 1830s, the name stuck: The French still refer to any clear soda as "limonade." *Courtesy of Cadbury Schweppes p.l.c.*

delicious flavorings by the 1850s. Although some operators still preferred the old-fashioned way of cooking up syrups from scratch, many began taking advantage of the manufactured flavor formulas now offered. From dozens of colorful bottles, fountain barkeeps poured imbibers an infinite selection, including old standards like pineapple, sherbet, raspberry, strawberry, wild cherry, orange, lemonade, root beer, ginger ale, coffee, tea, vanilla, and chocolate. For the more adventurous customers, there was mocha, kola, coconut, egg cream, maple, mead, walnut, catawba wine, and even champagne.

As soda fountain artisans experimented with the flavor palette now available to them, a few imaginative syrup combinations went beyond the norm and emerged as bona fide masterpieces of taste. One of the most notable mixtures to capture the public's ardor was concocted by University of Texas Medical School graduate turned pharmacist Charles C. Alderton. In 1885, he nudged the quiet passion of flavor mixing out from behind the counter when he tested various syrup and extract recipes at the Old Corner Drugstore in Waco, Texas.

Alderton witnessed the difficulty that some of the customers had when it came to choosing one flavor over another. He started combining some of these favorites in a single mix and eventually concocted the world's first "fantasia" blend. Delighted with the results, Wade Morrison, the drugstore's owner, offered the hybrid syrup as a regular choice at the fountain. Soon, customers were addicted to the delightful new taste, and it became the Old Corner Drugstore's biggest attraction. At the time, the drink lacked a formal name but locals knew how to get one: "Shoot me a Waco" was the call to order.

As word of mouth spread the news far and wide, competing drugstore operators wanted to dispense the flavor. To satisfy the expanding market, Morrison and Alderton mixed up the syrup themselves. But as the clientele of drugstores, soda parlors, and saloons who wanted to carry the flavor increased, they could no longer produce enough to keep up. Luckily, Texas bottler R. S. Lazenby came to the rescue. After some initial experimentation, he agreed that the Waco mixture was indeed a prime candidate for a large-scale bottling operation.

And so, the first bottle of Dr Pepper's Phos-Ferrates was produced by the Artesian Manufacturing & Bottling Company of Waco, Texas, in 1891. With little ill effect, the drink's famous local nickname was abandoned, and its popularity spread across the state. By the time the Old West became a memory, the unique flavor had trickled down to a national market of soda drinkers. With its moniker streamlined even further, Dr Pepper emerged as one of the mainstay beverages to survive

White Rock beverages ad, 1951
White Rock Products Corporation of Whitestone, New York, originally bottled mineral waters at Waukesha, Wisconsin. Begun in 1883, the firm went on to bottle many carbonated beverages, including White Rock Cola, Orange, Lemon-Lime, Raspberry, Root Beer, Saz-Rock, Cream Soda, and a Tom Collins Mixer. The delicate White Rock girl remained the symbol of these beverages for half a century. It's amazing that in 1951 she appeared bare-breasted in ads and on bottle labels! *Author's Collection*

THE WHITE ROCK GIRL *

*For over half a century—the symbol of America's Finest Beverages.

White Rock

SPARKLING WATER
PALE DRY GINGER ALE

WHITE ROCK COLA · ORANGE · LEMON-LIME · RASPBERRY · ROOT BEER · SAZ-ROCK · CREAM SODA · TOM COLLINS MIXER

Big Red Bottling Plant, 1947

R. H. Roark of Waco, Texas, began the Perfection Company as a barber and beauty supply in 1931. His partner, Grover Cleveland Thomsen, was a chemist and invented a soda pop formula using a mix of orange and lemon oils, vanilla, and red food coloring. In 1937, the company marketed Thomsen's brainchild: a bright-red flavoring they called Sun-Tang Red Cream Soda. In 1961, as the tale is told, Harold Jansing, president of a San Antonio bottling company, was golfing when he turned to his caddie and said, "Why don't you go get us a couple of those Sun-Tang Red Cream Sodas?" The boy addressed his own subordinate and shouted "Hey, go get us a couple of those Big Reds!" Later, Jansing told Roark about the event, and "Big Red" became the new name. Sales of the sweet, unforgettable treat soared high, and even today, Big Red remains a favorite, still being sold in forty states, the United Kingdom, Holland, Taiwan, Panama, and Tahiti. *Courtesy of the Dr Pepper Museum, Waco, Texas*

The Old Corner Drug Store, circa 1890

The Old Corner Drug Store was owned and operated by Wade Morrison in Waco, Texas, but medicine sales were not the store's main attraction: Inside was an elaborate soda fountain that drew a crowd. Everyone came to visit the biggest drugstore in Texas, including businessmen, housewives, farmers, and cowboys, and partake of the fountain's flavors. In 1885, a new flavorful syrup was added to the lineup, and customers ordered the fantasy beverage by saying "Shoot me a Waco!" In 1891, the new pride of the Old Corner Drug Store was named Dr Pepper. *Courtesy of the Dr Pepper Museum, Waco, Texas.*

Early "Home of Dr Pepper," circa 1906

Designed by Waco, Texas, architect Milton Scott, the Artesian Manufacturing and Bottling Company building was completed in 1906. In those days, horse-drawn delivery vans supplied by Wells Fargo Company Express delivered kegs of Circle A Ginger Ale from the "Home of Dr Pepper" to sales outlets in the state. Today, the Richardsonian-Romanesque edifice houses the Dr Pepper Museum and Free Enterprise Institute, the only non-profit organization dedicated to telling the story of the entire soft-drink industry. Inside, the museum features a soda fountain where visitors may indulge in sodas, sundaes, and milkshakes. Of course, Dr Pepper is the primary mixer. *Courtesy of the Dr Pepper Museum, Waco, Texas*

Charles C. Alderton, inventor of Dr Pepper

Medical school graduate Charles Alderton invented the "King of Beverages" in 1885. He was intrigued by the soda fountain and made the astute observation that customers had a tough time choosing flavors to mix with their carbonated water. He experimented with combinations and to his delight, created a "fantasia" blend that pleased the tastebuds. Wade B. Morrison, then owner of the Old Corner Drugstore in Waco, Texas, liked the taste so much that he offered it to local soda-sippers for sampling. Customers couldn't get enough, and before long, the complex flavor was the drugstore's pride. Today, an animatronic, speaking rendition of Alderton educates visitors at the Dr Pepper Museum in Waco. *Courtesy of the Dr Pepper Museum, Waco, Texas*

Clicquot Club song, circa 1926
As with many products in the 1920s, Clicquot Club had its own song. Radio was just getting started, and it seemed that everything under the sun was being advertised over the airwaves. At the same time, the public was yet unjaded by the songs they heard and snapped up every tune like irresistible ear-candy. As many are apt to do with information published on the Internet of the 1990s, radio listeners of times past took in all they heard and accepted it without debate. What could be more advantageous to a company than an actual song that was yodeled over product? In May 1926, the Clicquot Foxtrot March became the first radio theme song ever written for any sponsor. From 1926 until 1934, a dance orchestra called the Clicquot Club Eskimos remained on the NBC network. *Courtesy of Paul LaCroix*

the twenties, and with its signature flavor and bold image of individualism, it continued to satisfy customers for years to come.

The Acquired Taste of Moxie Nerve Food

In stark contrast to fantasy drinks like Dr Pepper, there were soda beverages that rose to prominence in spite of their taste. One of the most visible was Moxie Nerve Food, a curious drink that got a tenuous start in 1876 when Dr. Augustin Thompson of Lowell, Massachusetts, concocted an invigorating nerve tonic derived from the gentian root. Guaranteed to aid digestion, sleep, and calm the nerves (of course), it was originally created as a medicinal elixir to be taken by the spoonful.

As the product was being stocked by pharmacists, Dr. O. Phelps Brown described the gentian root's properties and uses in his 1875 book, *The Complete Herbalist*. Like many before him, he claimed that the root was a powerful tonic. It "improves the appetite, strengthens digestion, gives force to the circulation, and slightly elevates the heat of the body." Although considered to be quite "useful in debility, exhaustion, dyspepsia, gout, amenorrhea, hysteria, scrofula, intermittents, worms, and diarrhea," there was just one glaring negative to the magical gentian root: Its taste was purely, intensely, and permanently bitter.

Despite its unpleasant effect on the palate, Moxie Nerve Food endured and managed to develop a large and fiercely loyal following. In 1884, Thompson modified the nerve medicine by combining the syrup with carbonated water creating a tonic. The new version was called

Beverage Moxie Nerve Food and was first packaged by the Standard Bottling Company of Lowell. As demand grew, Thompson enlisted the aid of his sons to deliver the product and horse-drawn wagons emblazoned with the Moxie trademark soon became a familiar sight on the streets of Lowell. Moxie was fast becoming a favorite beverage.

Nevertheless, it was important to Thompson that his customers realize that Moxie wasn't made just for the pure enjoyment of imbibing. Instead, he emphasized the painstaking steps required to produce the extract from the gentian root and promoted its supposed health benefits. He warned customers that drinking Moxie might take some getting used to, but assured the uninitiated that they would find it "delicious and satisfying" after sampling just a few ice-cold glasses.

By 1885, the Moxie Nerve Food Company was formed, and its headquarters were stationed in Lowell. Thompson's son Frank E. took over the front office, and the company implemented an optimistic strategy of national expansion. At that time, efforts were made to deliver the drink to distant cities in states as far off as Colorado, Wyoming, and New Mexico. But the outreach program met with limited success. It wasn't until 1896 when Frank Archer joined Moxie that there was any real expansion.

Upon his arrival, Archer discovered that the Moxie firm was being restructured, and the company soon moved to Boston. There, the new building secured by the company proved advantageous for business, since hundreds of people passed it daily while on their way to the local railway station. Archer sized up the

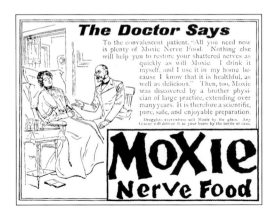

"The Doctor Says Moxie" newspaper ad, 1899

Moxie Nerve Food was advertised in newspapers as early as 1899 when the firm kicked off an ad campaign with a diverse cast of spokespeople, from tennis and golf players, to bicyclists, well-to-do yachtsmen, men of science, and most importantly—doctors. The core of the Moxie campaign was centered around children and their sick parents who needed respite from work. The wobbly letters in the Moxie logo (with the large "X") were used from the campaign's start and on into 1900: The shaky lettering reinforced the concept of Moxie as a nerve food. *Courtesy of Frank Potter*

"Drink Noxie Cola" postcard, circa early 1900s

Above: Noxie was a knock-off drink that latched onto the great success of Moxie. Almost exactly like the horse-drawn wagon used by the Moxie Company, the Crystal Springs Bottling Company of Waterloo, Quebec, used a Noxie Bottle Wagon to promote its knock-off. Even so, Moxie fiercely protected its widely advertised name and was successful in forcing copy-cats to cease and desist. Still, there remained a big thirst in Canada for soda pop: By 1946, consumption of soft drinks in Canada topped 55 million gallons (211 million liters) and more than doubled to 123 million gallons (468 million liters) by 1956. *Preziosi Postcards*

Moxie Bottle Wagon, circa 1899

Above, right: Before the 1900s, Moxie Bottle Wagons traveled from town to town in New England and were the chief means to promote Moxie Nerve Food. Kids far and wide recognized the Moxie wagons: At county fairs of the day, Moxie salesmen handed out small aluminum tokens to kids that were "good for one drink of Moxie," redeemable at a Bottle Wagon. Youngsters loved the shiny coins so much that they were often never redeemed. Boys kept them in their pockets as good luck charms, and girls had holes punched in them so they could be worn as pendants. *Courtesy of Frank Potter*

situation and proceeded to turn the company office into a giant advertisement. The exterior wall was painted a bright white and the trim a vivid green, while at the top of the facade, oversized brushwork proclaimed "The Moxie Company" in big, bold lettering.

From the flamboyantly decorated headquarters, Archer led Moxie into the twentieth century with a clever strategy to turn its unique taste into an distinct advantage. To achieve this lofty goal, all of the company's ads from the early 1900s blared "Learn to Drink Moxie." By the twenties, ads read: "It's the drink for those who are at all particular." Celebrities touted Moxie and hinted that it took

sophistication to acquire a taste for it.

And so, the brave act of acquiring a taste for a bitter soft drink resulted in a new addition to America's slang idiom. "Moxie" was originally a Native American place name, as in Moxie Falls, Maine, but it soon took on greater meaning in pop culture. From the soft drink born during the age of idols and ballyhoo known as the Roaring Twenties, the word "moxie" was universally adopted to describe traits like guts, pluck, and courage. As if by osmosis, Moxie had bubbled up and over into the pop culture lexicon where it went from an uppercase brand name to a lowercase noun. As one of the most unusual flavors from the fountains, it deserved nothing less.

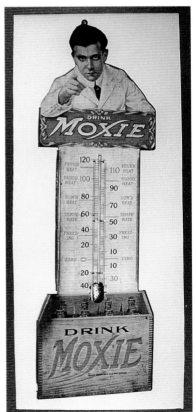

Moxie Brownies metal sign, circa 1905

Above, left: Moxie ads with the elfish Brownies played a role in giving birth to pop culture slang that is used even today. This metal sign with the embossed "Moxie" was manufactured by the M. D. Beach Company of Conshocton, Ohio, circa 1905. The Brownies were the invention of writer Palmer Cox: He received the inspiration for the imps from Scottish immigrant folktales he heard while growing up in Granby, Canada. The Brownie stories first appeared in *St. Nicholas Magazine* and were later published as an illustrated book. To give students extra recognition, teachers of the age showed their approval by rubber stamping small images of the Brownie elves onto exceptional school compositions. Eventually, the term "Brownie points" became so generic that the original connection was lost. Due to the elves' popularity, Moxie adopted the Brownies for its advertising. *Courtesy of Frank Potter*

Moxie bottles

Above, right: The Owens Automatic Bottle Machine debuted in 1903 and changed the way bottlers like Moxie packaged drinks. The new device made it possible to produce vast numbers of standardized and inexpensive bottles. Made in one piece, the bottles had a mold seam that extended through the bottle top and lip. Crown cork bottle caps (invented in 1891) were used to seal the opening. These Moxie bottles feature the 1907 logo in raised lettering around the bottle shoulder: The paper-label bottle (left) is circa 1914, the applied-color-label bottle (right) circa 1961. *Courtesy of Frank Potter*

Moxie thermometer, 1910s

Left: Moxie produced numerous colorful thermometers over the years to promote its brand. In the early days, point-of-purchase items like this were made of wood. This model featured a mercury tube held in place by three clamps, with the bulb protected by a perforated, metal cage. The crate below (with dovetail construction) was used during the early 1910s and held twelve bottles. *Courtesy of Frank Potter*

Moxie Horsemobile
Above: This is the sole surviving example of the famed Moxie Horsemobile, a fully restored 1929 LaSalle. Moxie Founder Frank Archer came up with the idea for the strange motorized equine and patented the "ornamental design for an automobile" in 1917. During Moxie's heyday, Horsemobiles were a bold promotional statement for the firm. This vehicle is now a fixture at Clark's Trading Post in North Woodstock, New Hampshire. It's pictured here in front of the Monarch Nu-Grape Company in Doraville, Georgia. *Courtesy of Frank Potter*

Moxie Fox Trot Song, 1930
Facing page: The "Moxie Foxtrot Song" debuted in 1921, and became a popular song and dance number. Without royalty payments, it was sung free of charge by soda pop fans across North America. This score was reissued in 1930, featuring one of the legendary Moxie Horsemobiles, this one built on a Rolls-Royce chassis. *Courtesy of Frank Potter*

Detroit's Drink Was Vernor's

Many Detroit hearts are warmed with the fond memories of a man, his ginger ale, and the mark he left on his city.
Keith Wunderlich, Vernor's collector

Vernor's Soda Fountain, 1947
In 1939, the worldwide revenues earned from the sale of bottled Vernor's and the flavoring extract allowed James Vernor to buy and renovate the ten-story Siegel Building in Detroit. In 1941, the facility was billed as the "most modern bottling facility in the world." In nearby Pontiac, Michigan, this tidy Vernor's Soda Fountain was operating in 1947. *Courtesy of the Keith Wunderlich Collection*

In 1858, James Vernor began his career in the soda pop business as an errand boy. He was hired on at the Detroit, Michigan, drugstore of Higby and Sterns at age fifteen and earned a reputation for tidy parcel wrapping and fast deliveries. At age nineteen, he enlisted in the Fourth Michigan Cavalry to fight in the American Civil War. Upon returning to Detroit in 1865, he built a livelihood on his former pharmacy skills and opened his own drugstore at 235 Woodward Avenue.

As was customary at the time, Vernor installed a soda fountain in his shop and proceeded to make a name for himself with a new beverage, Vernor's Ginger Ale. According to one account, the new syrup was concocted before he left for war, while employed at Higby and Sterns. Supposedly, he stored the extract in a wooden cask prior to enlistment; when he returned four years later, he was pleased to find that the aging improved the taste. But without documentation, most historians concur that it's more likely his first experiments began after the war. It was 1866 when Vernor first served the formula in a drink.

But while the timeline is questionable, devotees are unanimous in the fact that over the next decade Vernor's was refined. Striving for consistency, Vernor mirrored the rigid production standards that ruled his prescription-making operation: To enhance taste, the water was purified. In careful proportions, the Jamaican ginger that provided the flavor base was distilled and blended with a proprietary recipe of fruit juices. Even the carbonic gas that charged the soda water with its effervescent properties was custom made by the industrious Vernor.

For the next thirty years, the city of Detroit grew and so did the unique taste of Vernor's. By the time young James Vernor II joined the operation in 1896, the sublime ginger bouquet had attained a certain measure of greatness. Toiling sixteen hours a day, the father-and-son team made the drink—and their name—a household word. It was hard work: Along with clerical duties and prescriptions, they mixed the syrup, bottled the drink, and washed returned containers. During downtime, deliveries were made to retail outlets throughout the city.

Because of the workload, the elder Vernor decided to get out of the drugstore business and concentrate on producing ginger ale. The drugstore was closed, and a facility intended to blend, age, and bottle the Vernor's Ginger Ale was established at the foot of Woodward Avenue. Good fortunes poured out, and the manufacturing plant was a resounding success. Distribution was expanded, and horse-drawn Vernor's delivery wagons became a regular sight.

At the time, Detroit's busiest ferry docks were located at the base of Woodward, where commuters took the Bob-lo and Belle Isle boats to Windsor, Canada; additional excursion boats docked nearby. As a result, the location provided for a built-in customer base of eager imbibers. A steady stream of thirsty passengers stopped by on their way to and from work to tip an ice-cold flagon of Vernor's at the factory fountain. Later, a giant billboard at the point of entry illuminated the waterway between the two nations and accented Detroit's skyline like none before.

The public longing for Vernor's was insatiable. In town, all of the top drugstores installed special apparatus that exclusively dispensed Vernor's Ginger Ale. Interestingly enough, nearby hospitals picked up on the astringent qualities of the drink, and its use as a soothing palliative soared. After an enterprising soda jerk poured six and one-half ounces of Vernor's into one and one-half ounces of cream, downing a "Cream-Ale" became a fad. While the consumption in pharmacies rallied, thousands of bottles also were delivered to private residences by the caseload.

To meet the demand, Vernor and son expanded the business by making ginger ale extract that was sold to franchise bottlers outside Detroit. As part of the plan, Vernor purchased the old Riverside Power Plant and, in 1918, moved in his manufacturing setup. Two years later, he built a six-story office building next door. Unfortunately, he occupied the head office for less than a decade: With a life story equaling the greatest Horatio Alger tale, Vernor died in 1927 at the age of eighty-four.

As America entered the Great Depression, the Vernor's Ginger Ale legacy was passed down, and young James became acting president. Possessing his own knack for business, he took the James Vernor Company to new heights, turning it into a successful international organization. By 1939, the worldwide revenues earned from the sale of bottled Vernor's and the extract allowed him to acquire Detroit's renowned ten-story Siegel building and have it renovated to suit his requirements. In 1941, what was billed as the "most modern bottling facility in the world" was inaugurated at 239 Woodward Avenue.

Sadly, the boy who once helped his dad in the old drugstore passed away in 1952. J. Vernor Davis, the grandson of the founder, took over and named James Vernor III vice president. As a side effect of the restructuring, the company was forced to sell off some of its stock. While Davis boosted sales over the next decade, an ominous sign foretold trouble. Suddenly, the drink's name was changed to reflect less famil-

ial ties. With the apostrophe gone, "Vernors" became the domain of outsiders.

Appearing to be on top, the James Vernor Company celebrated its 100th birthday in 1966, and Davis was appointed chairman of the board. But things were not good: That year, Vernors was sold to a group of investors. By 1971, American Consumer Products bought it, and eight years later it was snapped up by United Brands. Hastily, they abandoned the Detroit facility and sold the property to a mall developer. By 1981, Vernors was for sale again and was picked up by A & W Brands. In 1993, the Cadbury Schweppes conglomerate assumed ownership of A & W and along with it, Vernors Ginger Ale. Saved by a stable company, it was finally rescued from soft drink oblivion.

Today, the ferries that docked at the base of Detroit's Woodward Avenue are gone, as are the billboards that touted the name, the fancy soda fountain dispensers that poured the drink, the etched glasses that overflowed with bubbling delight, and the playful gnome that adorned both the bottles and the ads. But don't ever tell residents of the Motor City to sip on a cola. "Deliciously different" until this very day, the drink of Detroit remains Vernors Ginger Ale. It always has been and always will be.

Vernor's Gnome die-cut, circa 1940s
Coca-Cola had its Sprite Boy, Clicquot Club its Eskimo, and Vernor's—a gnome? The Vernor's Gnome adorned much of the company's ads and bottles for years. With an impish quality, he had his own charm and became a familiar icon with Detroit citizens—and all those who loved the taste of ginger ale aged in wood. *Courtesy of the Keith Wunderlich Collection*

Vernor's Ginger Ale sign with Detroit skyline
James Vernor obtained Michigan's first pharmacy license. A perfectionist, he had high standards and attempted to work by them. Ahead of his time, he scrutinized prescriptions for quality, accuracy, and drug interaction! He served on the state pharmacy board and was the chief supporter of the state's first pharmacy law. Today, the Vernors soft drink name continues to survive—and satisfy. Schweppes is currently assisting in the renovation of a Vernor's mural in Flint, Michigan. This reproduction porcelain-enameled advertising sign features the cityscape of Detroit as seen during the heyday of Vernor's. *Courtesy of the Keith Wunderlich Collection*

Dr Pepper customer premium, 1900
Sellers of Dr. Pepper's Phos-Ferrates gave out this celluloid-covered memoranda booklet as a customer premium. While the detailed engraving of a water nymph may seem benign by today's standards, it was most likely viewed as risqué then. *Courtesy of the Dr Pepper Museum, Waco, Texas*

Dr Pepper "Sea Nymphs" lithograph, early 1900s
Known by Dr Pepper fans and ardent soda pop collectors as "The Sea Nymphs," this stunning lithograph promotional poster dates back to the early 1900s. *Courtesy of the Dr Pepper Museum, Waco, Texas*

"King of Beverages," 1900s
The 1900s saw beverage bottlers battling it out for the emerging market. Fresh, pretty faces—that could have been interchangeable among brands—vied for dominance at the local general store. One of the most overused scenes was the image of a well-dressed woman enjoying a glass of beverage. Curiously enough, this early Dr Pepper gal in low-cut frock exhibits a reserved, Mona Lisa–like demeanor. *Courtesy of the Dr Pepper Museum, Waco, Texas*

Dr Pepper syrup dispenser reproduction
Countertop syrup jar dispensers were used during the early 1900s. Fountain proprietors placed these units directly on the marble counter where the customers could see them, hence the "Drink Dr Pepper the Year Round" advertising. Able to hold one gallon (3.8 liters) of syrup, these ceramic beauties had an accurate measuring valve that allowed only one ounce (30 ml) of flavoring to flow through the spigot with each turn. As they were fragile, only a few survive today. This example is a reproduction on display at the fountain at the Dr Pepper bottling plant in Dublin, Texas. *Author/Dr Pepper Bottling Company of Dublin*

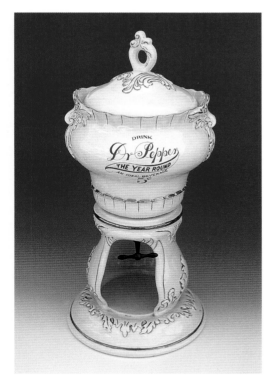

Jugging Dr Pepper fountain syrup, 1912
In 1912, Waco's Artesian Manufacturing and Bottling Company relied on hand labor to fill glass jugs with Dr Pepper syrup, label them, and pack them into shipping crates. The bottling plant became the Dr Pepper Company in 1923, and the headquarters moved to Dallas. The Waco plant closed in 1965. *Courtesy of the Dr Pepper Museum, Waco, Texas*

Drugstore fountain, circa 1910
The distinct "roses" lithographs decorating this fountain scene were distributed by Dr Pepper, and because Dr Pepper appears to be the main drink served, this establishment was in all probability located in Texas close to Waco's Old Corner Drugstore. Additional flavors were served here as well, evidenced by the row of hand-pumped syrup dispensers that neatly line the inside of the marble serving counter. With its overblown finial and festoon of paper promotional cards, the fountain used to dispense carbonated water takes prominence at the bar's center. *Courtesy of the Dr Pepper Museum, Waco, Texas*

Dr Pepper "Big Hat" lithograph, circa 1890s

Attractive faces were found to be an effective way to market product and gain attention in retail locations in the gay nineties, and the Dr Pepper "Big Hat" is yet another stunning entry in the long line of color promotions produced by the firm. Although the size and placement of the seller's trademark was less conspicuous in those innocent days, it was certainly present at the corner of the poster. *Courtesy of the Dr Pepper Museum, Waco, Texas*

Dr Pepper metal serving tray, circa 1909
A painted metal Dr Pepper serving tray featuring the slogan, "King of Beverages." *Courtesy of the Dr Pepper Museum, Waco, Texas*

Dr Pepper Vienna art plate, early 1900s
From 1909 to 1912, the Dr Pepper Company produced beautiful, metal art plates for decoration and promotion. The Vienna Art Plate Company was the primary maker of these Art Nouveau pieces (the firm also made many beautiful plates for The Coca-Cola Company), and today, only a few of these painted, gilded masterpieces remain. *Courtesy of the Dr Pepper Museum, Waco, Texas*

Pretty Peggy Pepper die-cut, circa 1940
Pretty Peggy Pepper didn't last but one year as an ad image. Dr Pepper unveiled her visage, but after World War II started, the company decided to promote the war in its ads. New promotions featured service men and women, and Peggy Pepper was promptly discontinued, only limited materials being made with her image. As a result, die-cut paper examples such as this one are rare commodities. *Courtesy of the Dr Pepper Museum, Waco, Texas*

Dr Pepper ranch scene die-cut

Above: Pretty girls and the lure of the wild West was a popular theme for selling soda and a format that Dr Pepper readily adopted. "Good For Life" began as a slogan in 1923 and was used up into the late 1950s. The red, shaded, tile-effect grid came out in 1934. Officially, the 1950 version of the company logo was the first to drop the period after "Dr.," dating this die-cut point-of-purchase piece somewhere in the late 1930s to 1940s. *Courtesy of the Dr Pepper Museum, Waco, Texas*

Dr Pepper 10-2-4 thermometer, circa 1930s

Left: "Drink a Bite To Eat at Ten, Two, and Four O'clock" was the idea of Erle Racey, a copywriter working for the ad agency Tracy-Locke-Dawson, Inc. The catchy slogan was inspired by the 1927 research of Walter Eddy, Ph.D., whose study indicated that human energy levels dipped at regular daily intervals. Racey submitted the phrase in a company contest and won seventy-five dollars for the effort. The Dr Pepper Company used the slogan for decades. *Courtesy of the Dr Pepper Museum, Waco, Texas*

Dublin Bottles with Real Sugar

My biggest thrill after all these years is the satisfaction I get from making Dr Pepper the old way and hearing the response from people who enjoy it like that.

W. S. Kloster, Texas bottler

Dublin Dr Pepper Bottling Company, 1996
In June 1991, the Dr Pepper Bottling Company of Dublin, Texas, planned to celebrate its 100th anniversary and honor the fact that it was the world's oldest remaining bottler of Dr. Charles Alderton's cherry-amaretto sensation. That morning, owner Grace Lyons passed on at age ninety-two. Later, longtime employee and soda pop enthusiast Bill Kloster learned that the entire outfit was bequeathed to him. With six decades of service, he became a fitting heir to the century-old tradition: "You work for a lot of reasons, but I guess my biggest thrill after all these years is the satisfaction I get from making Dr Pepper the old way and hearing the response from people who enjoy it like that." *Author*

In 1885, Charles Alderton created a soda drink he called Dr Pepper, and almost immediately, it became the favorite beverage at Wade Morrison's Old Corner Drugstore in Waco, Texas. For six long years, it was dispensed only at the local soda fountains, until the Artesian Manufacturing and Bottling Company was formed in an effort to bring the taste to a bigger market. At long last, all those who were thirsty for a "Waco" could purchase it in bottles, carry it home, and imbibe privately within the family parlor.

As Waco residents grew accustomed to Dr Pepper's increased availability, drugstore proprietor Sam Houston Prim and his wife were busy relocating from Sulpher Springs to Dublin, Texas. After settling in, they established a feed store, coal business, ice house, and a modest beverage bottling operation. To his credit, Prim acquired the rights to distribute Dr. Pepper's Phos-Ferrates within a forty-mile (64-km) radius of town and became the first operator outside of Waco to package the flavorful new refreshment.

Thirty years passed by, and the dream of making Dr Pepper into one of America's favorite soft drink sensations was realized.

When the Dr Pepper Company moved its national headquarters from Waco to Dallas in 1922, new franchise territories were offered. Since Prim was one of the original bottlers, he was given choice of the prime sales areas. With the comment "this will do for me," he spread out a map and drew a small circle around a fifty-mile (80-km) radius of Dublin, passing up far more promising regions.

In light of existing consumption, he wasn't far off the mark: Back then, soda pop was still a treat reserved for Sunday picnics and special outings into town. Four or five workers could easily produce the minuscule demand of fifty cases per day.

In 1933, W. S. "Bill" Kloster became one of those workers when he was hired on at the Dublin plant, working at age fourteen to help support his widowed mother and siblings. As a bottle sorter, he earned ten cents per hour. Although it wasn't obvious to him at the time, the "King of Beverages" held great promises for the future. And there was one added bonus: Since the elderly Prim never had a son of his own and Kloster had lost his father, the working relationship eventually transcended into a closer bond.

Content to be a big fish in a small pond, Prim passed away in 1946, leaving behind the bottling legacy for his spouse to run. When she died in 1959, Prim's daughter, Grace Lyon assumed an active role. By that time, young Bill Kloster had grown into a man and was well versed in all aspects of Dr Pepper production. In line with the late doctor's wishes, he was appointed manager. As the years went by, he rose to the challenge and emerged as a one-man marketing and sales force for the Dr Pepper brand, selling millions of cases of the industry's fifth-best-selling non-cola soft drink and the mystique.

His dedication to product integrity became

unflappable. When other bottlers switched from sugar to high-fructose corn syrup in 1979, he refused to adopt the cost-cutting measure. Today, he insists that only Imperial brand pure cane sugar will suffice. He regularly reminds the skeptics that Prim declared "we should never change the way we blend our sweetener with Dr Pepper concentrate." To make the dark brown syrup, three hundred pounds (135 kg) of the white granules are mixed with fifty-four gallons (205 liters) of the flavor base.

Now seventy-eight years young, Kloster still gets a gleam in his eye when he fires up the clanking, clattering bottling line every Tuesday morning. In spite of the numerous breakdowns and the hard to find parts, the vintage capping, washing, and sorting apparatus still manages to crank out six hundred cases of Dr Pepper every week. With all the precision of a reliable old clock, a steady procession of bottles parade off the production line where they are carefully slipped into crates.

To replenish the ever-dwindling stock of battered, returnable bottles, Kloster scavenges for leftovers whenever dealers leave the business. Nowadays, practical replacements may only be purchased from a Mexican glass manufacturer that requires a minimum order of $30,000. Consequently, the classic pop top containers with crimped bottle caps aren't distributed to any of the local convenience stores in Texas. Customers just aren't used to saving bottles for return and being reimbursed for the deposit.

With its use of original bottles and genuine sugar, the Dublin plant has attained the status of legend. Traveling to taste the wonders, the curious visitors who come from around the world aren't disappointed: Adjoining the bottling facility is Old Doc's Soda Shop, an old-time ice-cream parlor that boasts a marble bar and working fountain once used by Dublin Drug and Jewelry Company, where visitors may sample finished product.

From far and wide, hard-core Dr Pepper afi-

cionados make the Dublin pilgrimage to pick up their own personal stash—hauling away case after case of the wooden crates that cradle twenty-four returnable, refillable bottles. As the thirsty load vehicles, orders for the sugar-spiked recipe arrive by mail and phone.

With more than twenty-five thousand visitors passing through the facilities annually, it appears that loyal Dr Pepper drinkers are hooked on the way their favorite beverage used to be made. That's what the Dublin bottling works is all about: nurturing yesterday's bottling traditions while keeping alive the timeless qualities of taste and value. As long as the demand remains vibrant, Bill Kloster will do his best to make sure that the oldest remaining Dr Pepper bottling plant in the world will continue to thrive as a living, breathing testimony to what a little hard work, devotion, and a few hundred pounds of cane sugar can do.

Dublin Dr Pepper bottling line, 1996
At the Dr Pepper Bottling Company in Dublin, Texas, glass bottles are still filled with the original, pure-cane-sugar formula that made a Pepper taste so great in the good old days. Held together with bailing wire, 1930s-vintage bottling equipment cranks out the sweet treat every Tuesday on bottling day. Because it's too expensive to replace them, the bottles are now more expensive than the drink. A glass manufacturer in Mexico fabricates them, but the $30,000 minimum order makes their cost prohibitive. To make sure that the old bottle stock is returned, the plant only distributes to carry-out retailers within a forty-mile (64-km) radius.
Author/Dr Pepper Bottling Company of Dublin

The Regal Flavor of Canada Dry

John James McLaughlin, Canada Dry founder
Canada's most famous ginger ale, Canada Dry, got its start when chemist John James McLaughlin began experimenting with flavorings during the late 1880s. Today, the beverage and formula remain a favorite with soft drink consumers. *Author's Collection*

Canada's most famous ginger ale—Canada Dry—got its start when chemist John James McLaughlin began experimenting with flavorings during the late 1880s. Using the skills he learned at the University of Toronto's College of Pharmacy, he turned the mixtures born of his imagination into drinkable reality. Working out of a tiny carbonating plant in the city, he formulated improved versions of popular soda fountain libations of the day such as the lemon sour, sarsaparilla, cream soda, and ginger beer. Over time, the pursuit of a pale, dry, flavorful ginger ale consumed his passions.

While experimenting with different types of syrup flavorings, he sold soda waters in siphon bottles to make a living. But concoctions that were made on demand from carbonated water and flavorings were only lining the pockets of the druggist. McLaughlin had a vision: He dreamed of beverages that were formulated and packaged ahead of time. In order for him to realize the profits, pre-mixed drinks would have to be marketed as finished products to retailers.

Inspired, he moved his syrup manufacturing operations to a larger facility on Sherbourne Street in 1894. There he sought to improve his ginger ale currently being sold as McLaughlin's Belfast Style Ginger Ale. Attaining perfection wasn't easy; it would be ten years before an improved formulation of the drink debuted as McLaughlin's Pale Dry Ginger Ale. By then, the muddy hue of the drink's original recipe was lightened to a more appealing amber. The sweetness was diminished too, replaced by a sublime dry flavor. In 1905, a patent was filed for the new formula, and the name "Canada Dry Pale Ginger Ale" was trademarked.

As part of the new label design, McLaughlin intended to include a map of Canada as a background image. To complete the scene, a beaver, Canada's national emblem, was to take prominence. A problem surfaced, however: Canadian Pacific Railway was already using the beaver as part of its logo. Railroad officials requested that Canada Dry remove the paddle-tailed mammal from its label and keep it off. McLaughlin complied and replaced the mascot with a crown.

With an acceptable image established, Canada Dry was ready to be poured out across the border. To manufacture the product for export, plants were established in Toronto and Edmonton, and by 1907, the pale, ginger drink was being shipped to U.S. grocery jobbers and wholesalers. As more people tried it, a following was born. Later, prestige was bestowed upon the beverage when it was appointed to the "royal household of the Governor General of Canada," then the Duke of Devonshire. Having earned the adulation of royalty, the sparkling soft drink was touted as the "Champagne of Ginger Ales," and later, the trademark was emblazoned with a *golden* crown.

Sadly, McLaughlin basked in the glory for only a brief time. In 1914, he passed away at the age of forty-eight. At that time, his brother Sam assumed an active role in the company and moved to make it a thriving concern in the United States. Although current profits were modest, he was pressed by principals to invest heavy ad dollars in the American market. In a big way, consumers were to be informed that "Down from Canada Came Tales of a Wonderful Beverage." The investment paid off when Americans left dry by the Eighteenth Amendment and Prohibition began gulping ginger ale by the gallons. As a mixer, Canada Dry was just the ticket to mask the unsavory taste of bootleg Canadian whiskey or the homemade alcohol being distilled in speakeasies.

In 1922, the company set up a U.S. subsidiary as Canada Dry Ginger Ale, Inc. and opened a manufacturing operation in New York. But

"This ginger ale is light . . . dry, not filling. It keeps growing youngsters mentally alert, physically alive, perks 'em up in twelve seconds flat. Will not disturb mealtime schedules, it's so quickly, easily digested."—Canada Dry ad, 1960s

Mary Hartline and the carry-home carton ad, 1951
By 1951, companies like Canada Dry were promoting the idea of the carry-home carton. With the easily transported package, consumers could enjoy ginger ale not only as a mixer at parties, but at "meal time, snack time, and thirst time." *Author's Collection*

within a year, the entire company was sold. Ontario-born Canadian Parry Dorland Saylor bought all the assets for one million American dollars, and the Canadian company was now an American company, incorporated in Virginia. For the new owner, this change of venue proved to be a frugal move, since the United States had just increased import tariffs on ginger ale by 50 percent.

As the years passed, Canada Dry prospered, and more bottling plants came on line. In 1948, a fifth factory was opened in Vancouver, British Columbia, as franchise bottlers were approved by the company. Canada Dry was soon being packaged at soft drink operations throughout the Canadian provinces. But that was only the beginning: In 1953, Canada Dry became one of the first in the beverage industry to package its wares in cans. The introduction of sugar-free drinks followed in 1964, along with extensive use of radio and television for advertising.

In 1969, the company aired a series of comical television ads featuring a skinny, mustached actor dressed up as a Royal Canadian Mounted Policeman. As Sergeant Cash, it was his duty to ride his steed to visit U.S. supermarkets and hand over $100 bills to every housewife that could produce three Canada Dry bottle caps from her purse. Of course, this scenario didn't go over well with the Canadians—particularly the audiences in the Toronto area who were receiving the ads from nearby broadcasting stations in Buffalo, New York.

Always prepared to defend their reserved image, the mounties claimed that the ads were the worst thing to happen to their image "since Dudley Do-right, a red-coated dunce, fumbled his way through the Bullwinkle children's show." Nevertheless, the furor ended in 1970 when the commercials were pulled from the airwaves and never seen again. A few months later, the company removed the outline map of Canada from its label. Except for the longitude and latitude lines, no geographic features remained.

The demotion proved to be a harbinger of changes to come. By the 1980s, the company was passed along to numerous owners. First, it was bought by the Del Monte Corporation, an RJR Nabisco subsidiary; then, it was acquired by the Dr Pepper Company, followed by Norton-Simon Inc.; finally, it was purchased by Cadbury Schweppes p.l.c. for $230 million. And so, the tradition of providing a pale, dry ginger ale to North American consumers continued, uninterrupted. As was true when John J. McLaughlin first began, the famous Canada Dry shield continued to stand for the "utmost purity, sparkle and refreshing goodness."

Canada Dry logo, circa 1905
Below: For Canada Dry bottles, extract creator McLaughlin included a map of Canada as a background image for the trademark. Canada's national mascot, the beaver, was prominent at the center. Unfortunately, the Canadian Pacific Railway, who was already using the animal in its logo, requested that the mammal be removed as soon as possible, and it was. A crown served as replacement, and the regal lineage of Canada Dry was set in motion for future generations. *Author's Collection*

"Go Steady with Ginger," 1947
Facing page: "Go Steady with Ginger" was one of Canada Dry's famous ad campaigns. Published in color periodicals of the day such as the *Ladies Home Journal*, the ads aimed their sights on the youth market—the crowd that liked nothing better than smooth sailing and tingling refreshment. *Author's Collection*

GO STEADY WITH *Ginger!*

Your course is set for real refreshment when you sail along

with Ginger . . . with sparkling Canada Dry,

"the Champagne of Ginger Ales." There's nothing quite

like its breeze-fresh flavor, its tingling-crisp zest

to keep your spirits high. Make a date for

pure, wholesome enjoyment—*whenever*

you're thirsty. *Go steady with Ginger—*

Go steady with Canada Dry.

Ginger's always a winner . . . thanks to Canada Dry's Lloyd Liquid Ginger Process—the exclusive method for extracting all the natural goodness from pure Jamaica ginger.

GO STEADY WITH
CANADA *WORLD FAMOUS* DRY

"The Champagne of Ginger Ales"

Chapter 3

The King of Colas

*If, once introduced as a beverage in civilized countries, the demand
for it would soon become enormous. . . .*
The American Journal of Pharmacy, 1883

Coca-Cola ad, 1912
Facing page: The 1912 Coca-Cola ad campaign was the first to feature two models. This paper sign was printed by Ketterlinus Company of Philadelphia. Petretti's Coca-Cola price guide lists the value of this rare beauty at $2,500. *Courtesy of The Coca-Cola Company*

Coca-Cola syrup crockery jug, circa 1900
Right: Selling Coca-Cola syrup was a sticky business. It was the syrup salesperson's job to make sure that customers were not swayed to buy cheap, imitation cola syrups. Still, it was easy for hucksters to sway retailers since their products sold at half the cost of Coca-Cola. Multiple levels were incorporated into the syrup marketing system to insure that everyone profited. Still, it cost less than a dollar to produce a gallon (3.8 liters) of syrup. This gallon was sold to a wholesale grocer or druggist for $1.50. A fountain operator would buy it for $2. Since the jug yielded one hundred glasses (sold at a nickel each) the retailer made $3 on an initial investment of $2. *Courtesy of The Coca-Cola Company*

Post–Civil War Atlanta drew them by the hundreds: men, women, and children, all seeking a better life. They poured in from the devastated rural areas of Georgia and, together with Atlanta's citizens, forged a new alliance, rebuilding and strengthening the grand old city. Rising from the ashes of Union General William Tecumseh Sherman's flames, Atlanta was transformed into a bustling economic hub. This reborn entity was the city that brought together three key players in the saga of that king of colas: Coca-Cola.

Two of the major players were pharmacists, but their trade can in no way be compared to the professional field known today as pharmacy. In its American infancy, pharmacy was regarded as the duty of the treating physician. It was the doctor's responsibility to diagnose ailments, prescribe appropriate medicines, and finally dispense what was often his or her own medication. With scant training, physicians of the day sometimes served as an apprentice for a few years while those in a hurry merely assumed the title "doctor" and began practicing. Even those who attended colleges were believers in the treatments of the day: Bloodletting and cathartics (laxatives) were frequently prescribed. Often, the "cure" was more

John Styth Pemberton, Coca-Cola founder

John Styth Pemberton, the originator of Coca-Cola, was born in Knoxville, Georgia, in 1833; he moved to Columbus, Georgia, while a child. In 1869, he moved to Atlanta and established himself as a druggist. Several of his compounds gained a loyal following: Extract of Styllinger, Gingerine, Globe Flower Cough Syrup, Indian Queen Hair Dye, Triplex Liver Pills, and French Wine of Coca. Coca-Cola was born in May 1886, when Pemberton put the finishing touches on a new concoction that would serve as a day-time "pick-me-up" for the soda fountain crowd. Unfortunately, Pemberton died on August 16, 1888, before his new beverage became famous. He was buried in Columbus, and in his memory, Columbus citizens restored his boyhood home and built an authentic reproduction of an early apothecary shop. *Courtesy of The Coca-Cola Company*

painful than the disease, and it's no wonder the masses turned to self-treatment in the form of patent medicines.

To compound the problem, there were few pharmacology schools and even fewer laws governing the trade. With its laissez-faire entry requirements, pharmacy was a perfect career for charlatans eager to get rich on the other people's ills. Many of these fakes concocted and sold cure-alls laced with alcohol, opiates, and dangerous poisons. It was these unregulated nostrums that frequently caused physical distress and even death.

By the early 1800s, Samuel Thomson founded the Thomsonian System, a movement based on the rediscovered Galen theory of health. Neither a doctor nor a pharmacist, Thomson organized his teachings, patented his therapeutics, and gained a fanatical following. Unlike the medical status quo, his holistic rationale called on the natural elements of earth, air, fire, and water for healing. He used milder botanicals and therapies including lobelia emetics, scalding capsicum and herb teas, steam baths, and medicated enemas. (While these cures bordered on quackery, they did prompt study into the medicinal use of plants). By mid-century the movement waned, leaving behind a handful of splinter groups.

In 1850, nineteen-year-old John Styth Pemberton purchased a temporary physician's license from the Southern Botanico-Medical College in Macon, Georgia, an outfit run by one of Thomson's offshoot guilds. He enrolled, intrigued with the disciplines of botany and chemistry, and abandoned his plans of becoming a medical doctor in favor of pharmacology. Even so, Pemberton was so taken by the romance of being a physician that he adopted the nickname "Doc."

Pemberton's Search for a Winner

Upon completion of the course and award of his pharmacist's license, Doc Pemberton returned home to Columbus, Georgia. By this time, the quaint, physician-owned apothecary shop had all but disappeared from the scene. Restricted by new laws, general stores were now prohibited from selling drugs. As a result, there was a demand for skilled pharmacists who could create *and* dispense their own drugs. New standards outlined in the *U.S. Pharmacopoeia* and *National Formulary* boosted public confidence, dignifying the pharmacy profession in the public's eye.

In 1855, Pemberton opened a drugstore in Columbus under the name Pemberton & Carter. For the less ambitious person fresh from trade school, this might have been regarded as a more serious move, but for Pemberton the business was to be just a temporary measure. His real talent, discovered during his studies at college, lay in formulating new medicinal products.

Nevertheless, his aspirations would have to be delayed: The specialized paraphernalia needed to experiment was too costly, and the outbreak of the American Civil War in 1861 promised a climate unsuitable for tinkering. Without delay, Pemberton joined the Confederate Army and received the commissioned rank of lieutenant colonel. Upon discovering that he had a dislike for taking orders, he turned in his resignation papers. Not afraid to fight, he promptly organized two state militia units of his own and placed himself in command. Both units defended the town valiantly during the Battle of Columbus, and at war's end, the wounded Pemberton was esteemed as a local hero.

After the war, Pemberton returned to the kettle and percolator. His goal was to formulate a palatable elixir of his own design, a soothing concoction to capture the public's interest and earn him fame and fortune. While Pemberton dreamed, the future millionaires of patent medicine were already one step ahead, promoting their brand names by way of national ads, and suddenly, every ailment—from flatulence to malaria—had a sure-fire cure. Over the next five years, this endless parade of miracle cures spurred Pemberton's ambitions onward, but a lack of capital stood in his way.

In 1870, he embarked on a search for investors and traveled to Atlanta. It proved to be a fortuitous move: Pemberton discovered he had a knack for obtaining backers and over the next few years secured a stable of investors. Bolstered by the cash influx, he introduced Globe Flower Cough Syrup, his first elixir. Motivated by positive reactions from customers, he withdrew from the retail drug business and by decade's end devoted his full attentions to making his own proprietary products.

French Wine of Coca Debuts

While Pemberton was busy making a name for himself in the field, the second major player in the Coca-Cola saga reached Atlanta. In 1873, Asa Candler, a down-and-out man devoid of prospects but high on hope, stumbled into town. Like many others, the war had decimated his family's wealth and ended all hopes

of a decent education. Having served as an apprentice under two physicians in nearby Cartersville, Candler now decided to make his own way as a druggist.

Candler solicited a position at the various drugstores in Atlanta without luck; he even applied for a job at Pemberton's place but received the same rejection. Rather than beg for handouts, he forged ahead and was rewarded with a night clerk job at George Howard's store. With hard work and a keen sense for business, the industrious Candler was soon promoted to chief clerk.

About the time Pemberton's Globe Flower Cough Syrup debuted, Candler took the helm of his own shop. He found time to fall in love with the boss's teenage daughter and marry her, against Howard's protests. The disagreement didn't last long, and by 1882, Candler's connubial joining was accepted. Before long, Asa even joined in a business partnership with the old man. Four years later, Candler bought out his father-in-law and became the sole proprietor of the renamed Asa G. Candler & Company.

Meanwhile, Pemberton finally developed the elusive beverage he had dreamed of. It was a concoction inspired by one of Europe's favorite libations, the French wine-and-cocaine cordial widely sold as

Jacobs' Pharmacy, circa 1887
Willis Venable, the self-proclaimed "Soda Water King of the South," operated this twenty-five-foot (750-cm) marble extravaganza on the ground floor of Jacobs' Pharmacy. The first glass of Coca-Cola fizzed to life in May 1886, under the pillared canopy of this fountain counter. The unique blend of spices, citrus, and combined properties of the coca leaf and kola nut gave the drink its distinct flavor. The fountain continued its tradition of service to parched Atlanta citizens until early 1960. Later in the decade, the pharmacy was demolished to make way for a bank and office building. *Courtesy of The Coca-Cola Company*

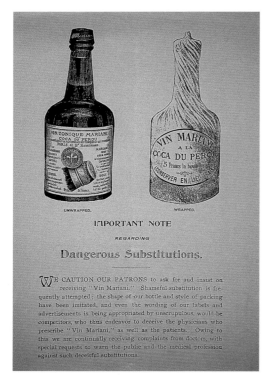

Vin Mariani ad, circa 1895
In 1871, a shrewd Corsican named Angelo Françoise Mariani developed a "nutrient tonic" made of coca leaves and Bordeaux wine. In the 1880s, he initiated an aggressive marketing program based upon the testimonials of world renowned celebrities by sending them gratis cases of Vin Mariani and inviting their comments. The body and brain restorative received praise from such notables as the Her Royal Highness Princess of Wales, Sarah Bernhardt, John Phillip Sousa, and Jules Verne. Mariani's success inspired dozens of competitors, among them being John Pemberton's French Wine of Coca, a facsimile of Mariani's formula. Little bottles of Pemberton's tonic made their debut in 1885 and received an overwhelming reception in Atlanta. In 1886, Pemberton developed his first batch of a new "brain tonic" based on coca and kola. *Warshaw Collection of the Smithsonian Institution*

Vin Mariani. Because the recipe was general knowledge in the trade, there were many imitators. Shortly after American drug maker Parke Davis & Company debuted a facsimile dubbed Coca Cordial, Pemberton unveiled his own version in the states and called it French Wine of Coca. Both beverages were received with great enthusiasm, which may not have been surprising considering the ingredients as listed by *The Standard Formulary*: Vin Mariani was made with 330 grams of sugar, 18 fluid ounces (540 ml) of alcohol (with red wine), and 1½ ounces (42 grams) of Coca leaf in powder form. Three daily dosages provided an exhilarating euphoria.

Although a single bottle sold for one dollar, Pemberton's French Wine of Coca received an overwhelming reception in Atlanta. With the ingredients needed to cure the public's "ills," sales soon exceeded several hundred bottles a day, and one Saturday, drink purchases topped eight hundred bottles.

To increase production, Pemberton moved operations to a more suitable structure. He found the perfect rental in the family home of Edward Holland, the son of an Atlanta banker. Strategically located, the red brick house on 107 Marietta Street was only three blocks from the city center. In December 1885, Pemberton set up a salesroom on the main floor, with office and storage upstairs. Both back room and basement were reserved for a manufacturing lab outfitted with a forty-gallon (152-liter) brass kettle, a tank, trough, and filter. A Matthews bottling machine was installed under the backyard coal shed.

The same month Pemberton was organizing his new digs, Frank Robinson and David Doe arrived in town with a printing press in tow. Former residents of Maine, the duo had been partners in numerous businesses. Eager to forget the raft of dubious deals they had left behind, they pooled their resources to open an ad agency. As a professional accountant, Robinson covered all the angles: Not only did he use all of his own finances, but he also invested the savings of his family and friends.

Coincidentally, the pair's first contact in town was a newspaper man who referred them to Doc Pemberton. Upon meeting, their personalities clicked, and soon Robinson, Doe, and Pemberton formed a partnership to create proprietary medicines. The newcomers would handle publicity, and Pemberton would oversee the duties of research and development. The agreement appeared to be so favorable that Holland joined as a fourth partner, putting up the title to his Marietta Street house. In January 1886, the business was incorporated as The Pemberton Chemical Company.

Building a Better Brain Food
Atlanta was not impervious to the latest fads and social amusements of the day. Its sweltering summer heat provided the perfect climate for soda fountains, the social rage of the century, and by 1886, the town boasted five outlets for bubbling refreshment. One of the finest was a twenty-five-foot-long (7.5-meters) marble extravaganza owned and operated by Willis Venable on the ground floor of Jacobs' Pharmacy.

On a warm spring day in 1886, a happy gathering of Venable's customers were enjoying the social amusements of lively talk and refreshing libation when

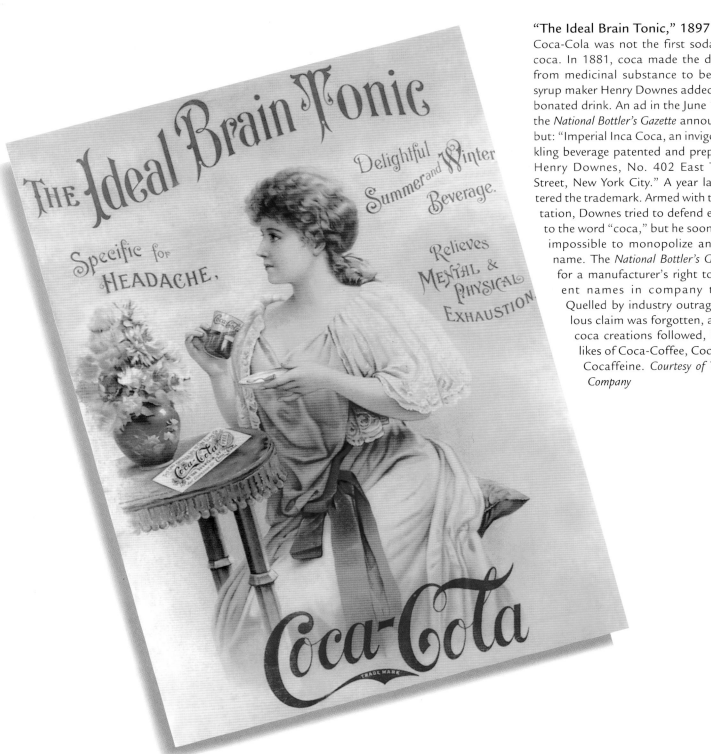

"The Ideal Brain Tonic," 1897

Coca-Cola was not the first soda pop to use coca. In 1881, coca made the dramatic leap from medicinal substance to beverage when syrup maker Henry Downes added it to his carbonated drink. An ad in the June 1884 issue of the *National Bottler's Gazette* announced the debut: "Imperial Inca Coca, an invigorating, sparkling beverage patented and prepared only by Henry Downes, No. 402 East Twenty-Fifth Street, New York City." A year later, he registered the trademark. Armed with the documentation, Downes tried to defend exclusive right to the word "coca," but he soon found it was impossible to monopolize an ingredient's name. The *National Bottler's Gazette* fought for a manufacturer's right to use ingredient names in company trademarks. Quelled by industry outrage, the ridiculous claim was forgotten, and a wave of coca creations followed, including the likes of Coca-Coffee, Coca-Malta, and Cocaffeine. *Courtesy of The Coca-Cola Company*

Wooden kegs of Coca-Cola syrup, circa 1920s
Above: In the early days of Coca-Cola, Asa Candler used secondhand whiskey barrels to store syrup. These barrels had to be clear (not charred), clean, white oak; old gin barrels were unfit as they had a paraffin coating. Because of the high volume of Coca-Cola sales, Candler had to develop methods for cleaning out the char, glue, and paraffin, and he directed that all used barrels be painted bright red to hide their vulgar origin. Finally, sales grew so high that the firm could not rely on a steady used barrel supply so new ones were made. The tradition of painting them red continued. *Courtesy of The Coca-Cola Company*

Early Coca-Cola bottling shed, 1914
Right: Many small bottling operations continued using old equipment until the crown stopper was adopted in the 1890s. Forced to update their bottling machinery, a good number cut corners in other ways. While this bottler sports an updated filling table, the bottling works is conducted in a converted barn. What's more, the bottle-washing department relies on an old hand-cranked soak-and-wash machine. *Courtesy of The Coca-Cola Company*

"Visit Our Modern Plant," circa 1930
In 1929, the American Bottlers of Carbonated Beverages turned to leading chemists in a quest for higher industry standards, and thus, a Voluntary Sanitary Code was published in 1929. It was the industry's hope that this new creed would encourage better bottling sanitation and assure consumers a safe, quality product. By 1930, stainless-steel equipment was developed, and new plants were the picture of cleanliness. This Coca-Cola bottling plant in Cambridge, Massachusetts, even encouraged public tours. *Courtesy of The Coca-Cola Company*

they were interrupted by an out-of-breath lad. Doc Pemberton himself had dispatched the messenger to Venable's fountain with samples of a strange new concoction. Always open to new flavors, Venable mixed up Pemberton's new syrup with carbonated water and served up free samples to all present. At first, tentative sips were taken, followed by approving smiles of appreciation as the sound of hearty gulps filled the room.

Upon first swallow, one could taste that this wasn't the usual mixture of ginger, sarsaparilla, root beer, or fruit commonly served at the average soda fountain of the day. Here was a multi-faceted flavor that was in a class by itself. Besides the great flavor, its invigorating quality was a pleasant surprise. Quite possibly, it could easily provide a cool, stimulating substitute for hot coffee and tea.

The search for a scintillating daytime beverage was not exactly a new one. The first of many additives to capture the imagination of syrup makers was the stimulant coca. First discovered by South American Indians, the leaves of the coca plant were mixed with lime and carried in a tiny bag during outings. By the late 1700s, coca's popularity resulted in a flourishing trade. The leaves were harvested by hand, dried in the sun, and packed into heavy bales for transport. In its heyday, the total annual Peruvian consumption of coca leaf topped seven million pounds (3.15 million kilograms).

Eventually, the coca leaf found its way to Europe where its properties as a stimulant and anesthetic became the topic of study. By 1860, German pharmacist Albert Niemann isolated the white crystalline, alkaloid cocaine. In Bohemia in 1884, Czech surgeon Carl Koller first used the powder as a local anesthetic. Only after Sigmund Freud advocated the substance's use in his writings was cocaine viewed as a drug, and it slowly gained an unsavory reputation. Years later, the Harrison Act of 1914 settled the cocaine controversy altogether by banishing it as an over-the-counter drug in the United States.

Nevertheless, it wasn't this concentrated alkaloid form of cocaine that was used in patent medicines or beverages during the 1880s. A less-potent extract was made directly from the coca leaves, which contained only minute quantities of all the chemical properties contained within the leaf (scientists later discovered that the leaves contained two other alkaloids of medicinal value, tropacocaine and hygrine).

During Pemberton's time, this tincture of coca was a popular ingredient in various patent medicines. Promoted as

Lillian Nordica premium, 1905
Above: In promoting Coca-Cola, the Massengale Advertising Agency of Atlanta used images of elegant men and women in majestic surroundings, as with this celluloid hanging sign framed in metal featuring American opera star Lillian Nordica. The early flare-tipped Coca-Cola glass on the gold pedestal fit this image, but unfortunately these initial glasses were top heavy with a tendency to tip over and break. By 1922, an improved bell-shaped glass replaced this model—subsequently replaced with the current version in 1929. *Courtesy of The Coca-Cola Company*

"All the World Loves Coca-Cola," 1904
Left: This advertising cutout appeared in 1904, years before the 1971 two-part harmony of "I'd Like to Buy the World a Coke." *Courtesy of The Coca-Cola Company*

Coca-Cola gal, 1908

Despite the fact that the Pure Food and Drug Act of 1906 barred food from being fraudulently labeled, this 1908 ad proclaims that Coca-Cola relieves fatigue! This may have been a reference to the sugar and caffeine content of the drink, which caused the company sticky legal problems. In 1909, the federal government seized a railroad shipment of Coca-Cola syrup in Chattanooga, Tennessee, and filed a lawsuit in federal court charging the company with criminal fraud. The feds had two charges against Coca-Cola: It was misbranded, since the name indicated that the product was made of coca and cola when it was not; and it was adulterated because it contained caffeine, then considered a dangerous drug. The trial began in March 1911, and within a month, the judge found in the firm's favor. *Courtesy of The Coca-Cola Company*

"whole body tonics," the potions that contained the essence of coca leaves were reputed to stimulate a healthy digestion, alleviate so-called female complaints, cure one's sexual debility, relieve depression, strengthen the blood, eliminate pain, and provide "food" for the brain and nerves.

Emergence of a Favorite Beverage

To differentiate his formula, Pemberton showed inventiveness with the addition of kola. Taken from the fleshy seeds of the *C. Acuminata* tree of West Africa, the stimulating kola nuts were first enjoyed by natives who chewed them for pleasure. In 1883, *The American Journal of Pharmacy* reported the nuts were used to form an invigorating drink throughout Africa and predicted that if it were introduced as a beverage in the civilized countries, the demand would be enormous.

Unfortunately, detailed chemical analysis revealed that the kola nut contained nothing more exotic than the stimulant alkaloid caffeine. As it turned out, it was just this sort of pharmaceutical grade caffeine that became the primary stimulant in Doc Pemberton's syrup. Because kola and coca extracts were costly, Pemberton added as little as he could, reducing the quantity to a minuscule level. To mask the inherent bitterness of the two, a unique blend of spices and citrus flavorings were carefully mixed in.

For a proper product name, Frank Robinson seized the day: He combined the names of the main ingredients of the syrup and suggested the word combination "Coca-Cola." With a name chosen, Pemberton's soda syrup debuted with an official announcement in the *Atlanta Jour-*

Coca-Cola coupon, circa 1900s
Right, top: Devised by Frank Robinson during the Pemberton days, free-sample tickets were a great way to introduce soda fountain patrons to the refreshing, invigorating qualities of Coca-Cola. Evidently, this "try it before you buy it" method paid off handsomely: By the year 1910, syrup sales to soda fountains hit 2,864,973 gallons (10,886,897 liters). *Courtesy of The Coca-Cola Company*

Coca-Cola blotter, 1904
Right, bottom: Paper products have always been an inexpensive and stylish medium for advertising. Coca-Cola made a variety of colorful pieces in paper, including blotters, bookmarks, and coupons. Blotters were the most popular. Their handy size and shape were the perfect canvas for colorful illustrations, ad slogans, and product information. *Courtesy of The Coca-Cola Company*

nal on May 29, 1886. For those who frequented the local city soda fountains, the ad copy was intriguing: "Coca-Cola. Delicious. Refreshing. Exhilarating. Invigorating. The New and Popular Soda Fountain Drink, containing the properties of the wonderful Coca plant and the famous Cola nuts. For sale by Willis Venable and Nunnally & Rawson."

Ironically, the new Coca-Cola drink had barely made a splash in Atlanta's soda circles when tragedy struck: Plagued by chronic stomach problems, old Doc Pemberton suddenly fell ill. Because the ailment was serious, production of his new soda syrup came to a halt, and the promising fountain season of 1886 pro-

General store with signs, circa 1920
During the 1910s and 1920s, Coca-Cola—and the signs that advertised it—became a highly visible part of roadside America. To sell beverages, tin signs, wooden placards, and thermometers were all part of the typical general store scene. Back then, the names of the stores weren't nearly as important as the many brands of familiar merchandise that were sold inside. *Library of Congress*

duced only a meager twenty-five gallons (95 liters) in sales. Disgusted, David Doe pulled out of the arrangement and left town, taking the color printing press that he and Robinson had arrived with.

Robinson's belief in the future of Coca-Cola was unwavering, and he elected to stay on. During the lull between fountain seasons, he worked intensely on further refining the syrup logo. By fall 1886, his tireless efforts were rewarded with that perfect specimen of penmanship now epitomized by the flowing letters of the Coca-Cola trademark. The following spring, Robinson was joined by Pemberton (who briefly had regained his health), and they were ready to tackle the new soda fountain season.

Robinson's marketing strategy was simple: If you can't get the product to the people, then get the people to the product. First, coupons were passed out for two free glasses of Coca-Cola. Concurrently, signs were posted throughout Atlanta. To spread the word, the Pemberton Chemical Company hired salesman Woolfolk Walker to carry the flavorful news of Coca-Cola beyond the city limits of Atlanta. Thanks to Walker, orders poured in from nearby settlements, and soda fountain operators were besieged by rising demand. Buoyed by the developments, Pemberton registered the Coca-Cola insignia and was granted the trademark for Coca-Cola Syrup & Extract in June 1887.

That summer, Pemberton's failing health worsened. In need of funds, he called old friend and patent medicine salesman George Lowndes to his bedside. Desperate, Doc offered him and fountain operator Venable a two-thirds share of Coca-Cola in exchange for a $1,200 loan. Venable would be the working partner and Lowndes the backer. The agreement was formalized on July 8, and as Pemberton neared death, all ingredients, equipment, and advertising were moved to the basement of Jacobs' Pharmacy.

Despite their efforts in the birth and marketing of Coca-Cola, Edward Holland and Frank Robinson received no compensation at all. Enraged, Robinson sought out the services of John Candler, a young lawyer of Mr. Holland's acquaintance and unrelated to Asa Candler. John Candler called on the dying Pemberton and reported back that Robinson didn't have a case. According to the words of a dying Pemberton, the formula for Coca-Cola never belonged to the Pemberton Chemical Company. What's worse, old

Doc was now a pauper.

Meanwhile, the future of Coca-Cola wasn't looking so bubbly. Venable was far too occupied with his fountain operation to take time to produce the syrup. When Lowndes confronted Venable, he agreed to produce more. After Venable neglected to uphold the promise, a dispute erupted. Angered over the stagnation, Lowndes embarked on the task of selling out his— and Mr. Venable's—financial interest.

With no takers, Lowndes approached Woolfolk Walker, the crackerjack who had done such a great job for Pemberton Chemical. Unmoved by the offer, Walker announced that he, like others connected with Coca-Cola, didn't have a dollar to his name. Despite Walker's reluctance, Lowndes posed an intriguing scenario: Walker could drum up backers and raise $1,000 to buy out the Coca-Cola name and equipment. Later, he could pay out the remaining balance from future profits.

Around that time, Walker's sister had sold her home in Columbus and was preparing to buy another in Atlanta. Employing his persuasive skills, the good brother convinced his sibling to invest her nest egg of $1,200. In December 1887, the Walkers became the second owners of two-thirds interest in Coca-Cola. Once again, all equipment, ad stock, and inventory were moved. This time, it was headed back to the basement of the Pemberton Chemical Company for temporary storage.

Improving the Coca-Cola Formula

All of these financial wheeling and dealings had not gone unnoticed by Frank Robinson, who steadfastly believed that

WELDMECH *FULL STREAMLINE* **BOTTLERS' SEMI-TRAILER BODY**
Capacities 180 to 325 Cases or More

Delivery truck, circa 1930
Uniform truck colors were adopted by a Coca-Cola Standardization Committee in 1925: All vehicles were required to be yellow and red, with black hoods, fenders, and radiators. During the 1930s and 1940s, the Weldmech Steel Products Company of Hattiesburg, Mississippi, made "full streamline" trailer bodies for soda pop delivery trucks. This handsome unit boasted a sign box for carrying road signs, a rear bumper, torpedo-type running boards with one-piece pressed-steel drop panels, crown fenders, and lights in the rear panels. Room was allotted for display of the brand name both at the trailer top and rear. *Preziosi Postcards*

he would play a role in the future of Coca-Cola. Robinson got a job at Asa Candler's shop. He would point to wagons loaded with empty beer kegs and predict to Asa that someday there would be wagons laden down with casks of Coca-Cola. Candler wasn't impressed by the brash prediction of his employee and shrugged off the comment. Unexpectedly, his thinking changed in summer 1888 while suffering from indigestion and a headache. As fate had it, he was at Venable's soda fountain that day and sampled his first glass of Coca-Cola—and gained immediate relief! (From today's perspective this miraculous cure is not surprising as caffeine is used in headache rem-

1899-1902   1900-1916   1915   1957   1961   1991   1994

Coca-Cola bottle progression, 1899 to 1994

Above: Despite advances in bottling, washing returned bottles in the early days of soda pop was problematic. Without automation, the cleaning process was defined by a syrup barrel (sawed in half), some water, and cheap labor. Visible dirt was removed first and then bottles were rinsed. The rinse water was often dirty, since each batch cleaned four or five cases. Fortunately, there were some bottlers who soaked returned bottles in a caustic solution of potash. Cleanliness became even more difficult with the introduction of the Hutchinson stopper, as it obstructed attempts to insert a brush into the bottle neck. It was necessary to put lead shot into the bottle and shake it so that hardened dirt could be loosened and rinsed out. *Courtesy of The Coca-Cola Company*

The shape that almost was, 1913

Right: In 1913, the Root Glass Company of Terre Haute, Indiana, entered a bottle design contest sponsored by Coca-Cola bottlers. Seeking inspiration for a unique design, plant superintendent Alex Samuelson sent a company accountant to the library for information on the coca bean and kola nut. He returned with an intricate line drawing of what he thought was the coca bean. He had made a mistake: The picture actually showed a *cocao* bean! Call it fate, luck, or chance, but that simple mistake resulted in the famous green-tinted bottle with those familiar curves. Root's mold shop supervisor, Earl Dean, produced prototypes based on the cocao bean drawing. Despite the fact that the bottles completely captured the image of the curvaceous bean, the stylish curves and ridges proved too voluptuous for the standard bottling equipment of the day. The prototypes were rejected. Only two of these original Dean prototype bottles are known to exist today. *Courtesy of The Coca-Cola Company*

Coca-Cola cone-top can, circa 1930

Below: Coca-Cola experimented with a metal cone-top can during the 1930s. So that consumers wouldn't be shocked, these odd, new-fangled containers were displayed at stores alongside standard glass bottles. Although the thirty-two-ounce (960-ml) can and its sixteen-ounce (480-ml) sibling (not shown) were a great concept, the high costs of manufacture stifled an industrywide switch. The public was cool on the can as well, and it wasn't until after World War II that it saw widespread use. *Courtesy of The Coca-Cola Company*

Coca-Cola *Verfrischend* stand in Amsterdam, 1928

Above: The roots of Coca-Cola during the early years of international expansion were similar to the early days of root beer stands in the United States. Here, three Dutch servers greet thirsty passersby with a universal thirst quencher, ice-cold Coca-Cola. *Courtesy of The Coca-Cola Company*

Coca-Cola take-home carton, circa 1930s
In 1922, Coca-Cola's Harrison Jones had a vision of the six-bottle carton and saw it as a means to get Coca-Cola into more homes. At the time, transporting Coca-Cola by the caseload was cumbersome, and there was little doubt that a smaller pack of six that sold for twenty-five cents would be a hit. And so, the six-pack carton was introduced in 1924. While slow to catch on at first, the so-called "handle of invitation" was picked up by seventy million Americans by 1939. *Courtesy of The Coca-Cola Company*

Copycat Coca-Cola logos
Early studies led researchers to believe that the strange-looking kola nut contained properties similar to coca leaves. When used as the basis for a whole-body tonic, pharmacists viewed the nut extract as a miracle substance capable of banishing fatigue and increasing alertness. It was an invitation for pharmacists—who comprised the bulk of early soda fountain operators—to make kola a key ingredient in their soda creations. For Coca-Cola, this proved a great problem as competing brands emerged with similar cola names. The trademark was fiercely defended, and eventually, all the copycat cola creators disappeared from the scene. *Courtesy of The Coca-Cola Company*

edies, and carbonated water is known to assuage dyspepsia).

With his business acumen, Candler recognized the marketing potential of a drink that was both refreshment and restorative. Impressed by this marvelous beverage called Coca-Cola, he set out to acquire sole ownership. It didn't take long: By canceling an old debt of $550, Candler procured Pemberton's one-third share. After he purchased another one-third share from Woolfolk Walker and his sister for $750, Candler possessed the two-thirds majority required to make the decisions.

As Coca-Cola was positioned for greatness, John Styth Pemberton's life waned. That summer, the old Doc finally succumbed to his illness. On August 16, 1888, he died at the age of fifty-seven, never conscious of the final destiny his drink would attain. On the day of his passing, a hush fell over Atlanta. In honor, the town's druggists closed up and gathered in memorial at Candler's shop. Presiding over the group, Candler spoke reverently of the Doc's "lovable

nature," adding a final epitaph that was short and sweet: "Our profession has lost a good and active member." Before the dirt on Pemberton's grave had settled, the Coca-Cola equipment was transferred to the basement of Candler's drugstore.

Because of customer complaints about spoilage, Candler and Robinson turned their attentions to improving the formula's stability. After trial and error, they remedied the preservation problem by adding glycerin as a stabilizer. At the same time, they removed the citric acid that Doc had used as a preservative and increased the phosphoric acid to add zest. The taste of the original required some refinement too, so they tinkered with the ingredients—adding and subtracting until they achieved satisfactory results.

On April 22, 1891, Candler was finally able to secure the remaining interest in Coca-Cola. The final third held by Woolfolk Walker and his sister was snatched up for $1,000, making Candler the sole owner of all rights and patents. The timing proved to be perfect: By the end of the summer, the commercial sales of Coca-Cola syrup jumped up to 19,831 gallons (75,358 liters). When the drink acquired the friendly sobriquet "Coke" with southern soda sippers, Candler realized that the time was right to expand operations.

With Candler as president and staunch advocate Frank Robinson as secretary, a reformed Coca-Cola Company was incorporated on January 29, 1892. To raise the capital he needed to enlarge his existing factory, add delivery vehicles, and hire salesmen, Candler sold his drug business for $50,000 and went public with the sale of Coca-Cola stock, issuing 1,000 shares valued at $100 each. Candler paid for half and gave 10 to Robinson. The remaining paper was offered through East Coast brokers. Although a brave Bostonian by the name of F. W. Prescott purchased 75, the remaining 415 went unsold.

Undaunted, Candler rolled up his sleeves and began to make his mark on the world with Coca-Cola. During the first difficult years, he plowed all of his profits back into the company—hoping to ensure its financial success. Along the way, he steadfastly defended the reputation of Coca-Cola in several court battles and fiercely protected the trademark and the quality that it stood for. For the next twenty-four years, he spent his life at the helm of a beverage company that few initially had any faith in.

By the time Asa Candler went into retirement in 1916, innumerable kegs of Coca-Cola syrup could be seen moving along the roadways, railways, and waterways of America. Frank Robinson's vision of syrup-laden delivery wagons trundling along Atlanta's streets had been surpassed. In 1919, the sale of The Coca-Cola Company went far beyond the wildest dreams of any of its originators, netting a fortune of $25 million. Now—headed by Ernest Woodruff—the company ushered in an exciting era of expansion. Coca-Cola was on its way to becoming a major part of American "pop" culture.

Baird's Coca-Cola clock, circa 1896

The Chicago-era Baird Clock with an eight-day movement was made between 1896–1900 and offered as a premium for high-volume dealers of Coca-Cola syrup. It's a curious promotional example, as it reflects the ambivalence that Coca-Cola portrayed in some of its early advertising: While it extols a "refreshing beverage" with one slogan, another cites its use as a "headache and nerve tonic." It wasn't until 1904 that Coca-Cola abandoned all medicinal references and staked its claim exclusively on refreshment. *Courtesy of The Coca-Cola Company*

Generations of Coca-Cola Ads

First known Coca-Cola ad, 1886
Top, left: Historians may never know for sure if John Pemberton received the inspiration for his stimulating coca beverage from writings of the day or from the influence of other products. Considering the ingredients he used (and the first ads promoting Coca-Cola), it's clear that his purpose was to produce a daytime pick-me-up. And a pick-me-up it was, since a single glass of the prototype formula provided the stimulating effect of 1½ cups (375 ml) of strong (and sweet) coffee! *Courtesy of The Coca-Cola Company*

Knitting girl, 1919
Top, right: Printed in the *Woman's Home Companion* picture section in May 1919, this typical Coca-Cola ad of the period follows the format of the company's yearly color calendars, albeit in monochrome. A pretty girl taking part in a relaxing pastime while enjoying a glass of Coke was a simple and effective sales vehicle for that day—and today. *Author's Collection*

"A Star Drink," 1906
Bottom, left: Atlanta's Massengale Advertising Agency placed this full-color ad on the back cover of the *Theatre* magazine, June 1906. Sitting at her makeup table in full costume, this actress or singer enjoys "full service." During this period, both the Massengale and D'Arcy ad agencies were employed by Coca-Cola. To distinguish the two, Massengale signed its ads, and D'Arcy placed a "D" with an arrow through it in its ads. *Courtesy of Michael Dregni*

"A wonderful girl in a real American pose," 1925
Bottom, right: The *Ladies' Home Journal* was one of America's first periodicals dedicated solely to women. A good example of clever copywriting, this ad shied away from staged poses and settings, relying instead on the honest picture of a girl in a "real American pose," sitting at the soda fountain, satisfied. *Author's Collection*

"The charm of purity," 1938

Left: "Here's the way to feel refreshed" was one of many Coca-Cola ad slogans. In 1938, the year this ad was in use, a bottle of the drink could still be bought for a nickel. *Author's Collection*

Housewife and six-bottle carton, circa 1949

Below, left: In 1876, paying out $75 for bottle-washing equipment was viewed by the industry as outlandish! By 1965, this attitude changed, and the cost of a basic bottle washer reached $80,000. With the capacity to wash five hundred bottles a minute, bottlers found it easy to cycle through the returns and restock the shelves as quickly as possible. Without ample resources to clean and process bottles, the high-volume sales promoted in ads like this one would not have been possible. *Author's Collection*

"Things Go Better with Coke," 1965

Below, right: By the 1950s, the naive themes of Coca-Cola's early decades were but a faint memory. Modern motifs dominated the ads in national magazines, and women were at long last being portrayed as more than mere product models—although sexual stereotypes certainly remained. Coca-Cola was a drink that accompanied all life's activities, including having your hair done at the beauty salon. *Author's Collection*

German Coca-Cola ad, circa 1930s

Above, left: "Your Future in the Coca-Cola Business" was an ad slogan printed in German trade periodicals during the post–World War I campaign to promote the worldwide use of Coca-Cola. *Courtesy of The Coca-Cola Company*

Eiskalt Sprite boy, circa 1940

Above, right: Around 1940, artist Haddon Sundblom used his own face as a model in order to revamp a Walt Disney version of the elfin face known as "Sprite." Unfortunately, the public nicknamed the little imp "Cokie," and this was frowned upon by the legal Coca-Cola department, which feared it would lead to trademark problems. As a result, Sprite was quietly retired, popping up for an occasional appearance during special promotions. *Eiskalt*, or "ice cold," were the words that accompanied his smiling face in German ads of the day. *Courtesy of The Coca-Cola Company*

Coca-Cola thermometer, circa 1941

Right: The year 1941 was one of change not only for the United States, but also for The Coca-Cola Company. The year began with an unprecedented Coca-Cola ad budget of over $10 million. In addition, the drink's popular nickname "Coke" became accepted, making its appearance on bottles in December. The December 8 attack on Pearl Harbor prompted The Coca-Cola Company's president to announce: "We will see that every man in uniform gets a bottle of Coca-Cola for five cents wherever he is and whatever it costs." *Courtesy of The Coca-Cola Company*

Katzenjammer Coca-Cola ad, circa 1927
The sentiment in this German Coca-Cola advertisement is equal to a 1927 American version that states: "For that tired, discouraged feeling—drink Coca-Cola." *Courtesy of The Coca-Cola Company*

"Drink Coca-Cola" sign, circa 1920
The famous Spencerian script was originally penned by Frank Robinson, Pemberton's partner and bookkeeper. When Coca-Cola reached its second home at Jacobs' Pharmacy in July 1887, part of Pemberton's inventory included a stencil plate with the words "Coca Cola," sans hyphen. Robinson combined the names of the two main ingredients, the coca leaf and kola nut, and he spelled kola with a "C" to gain a more pleasant appearance in ads. Shown is a circa 1920 Coca-Cola cardboard sign with metal frame and two 1916 bottles. *Courtesy of The Coca-Cola Company*

Coca-Cola Calendars Through the Years

Hilda Clark calendar, 1903

Top: Coca-Cola calendars often featured celebrities of the day, including vivacious singer and actress Hilda Clark. The elegant Clark first posed for lithographic art in 1899, and several versions of her image were used by Coca-Cola and the Massengale Advertising Agency until 1904. This Coca-Cola calendar was printed by Wolf & Company of Philadelphia, Pennsylvania. *Courtesy of The Coca-Cola Company*

"World War I Girl," 1916

Bottom, left: The so-called "World War I Girl" appeared circa 1916 on the Coca-Cola calendar and on a separate change tray. In the same pose and dress, she held a bottle of the beverage on the calendar and a small glass on the tray. *Courtesy of The Coca-Cola Company*

"Cleopatra," 1928

Bottom, right: The beautiful and wholesome "pretty girl" image was always a matter of pride for Asa Candler and The Coca-Cola Company. Since the first inception of the calendar series in 1891, these color-rich lithographs were intended to invoke a quiet sense of elegance and modesty. However, individual bottlers viewed the medium quite differently, and as a result, they produced their own interesting—and often risqué—lithos of questionable taste to the age. *Courtesy of The Coca-Cola Company*

94

Norman Rockwell calendar, 1931

Above, left: Famed artist Norman Rockwell captured a number of purely American scenes on canvas for The Coca-Cola Company. In 1931, the company's annual advertising calendar featured one of Rockwell's classics, an innocent "Tom Sawyer" scene. *Courtesy of The Coca-Cola Company*

"Your thirst takes wings," 1941

Above, right: The always colorful Coca-Cola advertising calendar flies high for the war effort in 1941. *Courtesy of The Coca-Cola Company*

"There's nothing like a Coke!" 1956

Bottom, left: With an updated bathing beauty wearing the latest in seaside garb, The Coca-Cola Company's long-running calendar girl series takes a trip to the beach. *Courtesy of The Coca-Cola Company*

"The Pause That Refreshes," 1963

Bottom, right: The California surfing craze of the 1960s influenced the Coca-Cola calendar. Coca-Cola was a needed supply for every surfing safari. *Courtesy of The Coca-Cola Company*

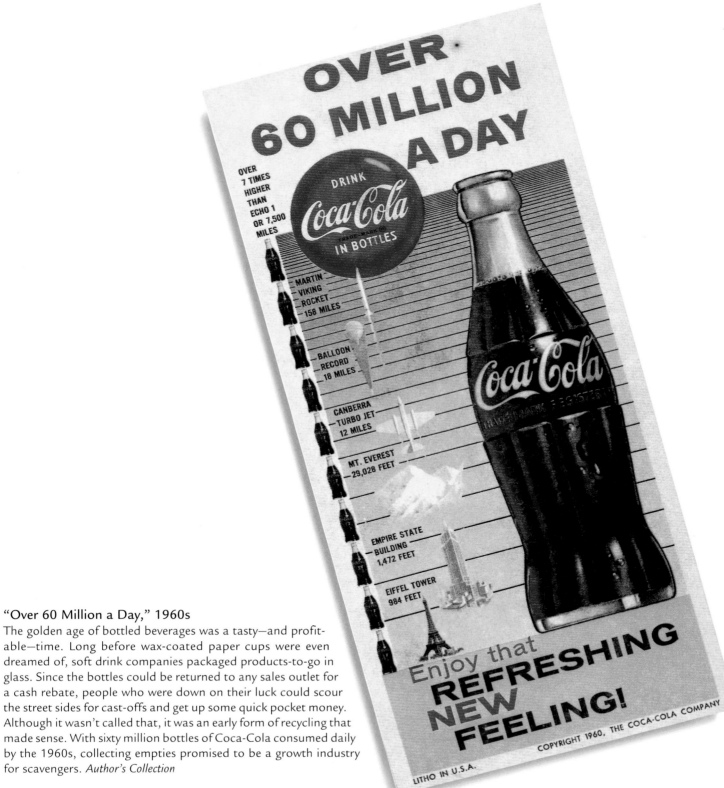

"Over 60 Million a Day," 1960s

The golden age of bottled beverages was a tasty—and profit-able—time. Long before wax-coated paper cups were even dreamed of, soft drink companies packaged products-to-go in glass. Since the bottles could be returned to any sales outlet for a cash rebate, people who were down on their luck could scour the street sides for cast-offs and get up some quick pocket money. Although it wasn't called that, it was an early form of recycling that made sense. With sixty million bottles of Coca-Cola consumed daily by the 1960s, collecting empties promised to be a growth industry for scavengers. *Author's Collection*

Mopheads, 1960s

Above: Print ads, radio spots, and TV commercials were only some of the ways Coca-Cola and other drinks gained fame. While much of pop's future was planned from the beginning, its destiny was fixed by those unexpected incidents that often propel a product into the limelight. Chief among these happy accidents were the impromptu, unrehearsed testimonials of prominent figures. If you could catch a president, pop star, or baseball hero downing a drink and freeze the moment in a photo, your sales were sure to rally. When the Beatles landed in the United States and refreshed their thirst, they were fair game for the paparazzi. *Courtesy of The Coca-Cola Company*

JFK smiles for a Coke, 1960s

Left: President John F. Kennedy was captured on film with the ubiquitous bottle of Coca-Cola. During the 1960s, a soda pop company couldn't ask for a better affiliation. *Courtesy of The Coca-Cola Company*

"Délicieux," circa 1940

American ads of the 1940s and 1950s that featured people enjoying leisurely activities—such as playing tennis—were duplicated for many of The Coca-Cola Company's foreign markets. Like other nations, the French were informed of the "delicious" qualities of the Coca-Cola beverage with simple words and colorful images. *Courtesy of The Coca-Cola Company*

"Victorian Girl" serving tray, 1897

Below, left: In 1907, the D'Arcy Advertising Agency took over the majority of the Coca-Cola advertising from the renowned Massengale firm. The first order of business was to upgrade the "pretty girl" image that had come to be synonymous with Coca-Cola. While the theme of elegant women posed with the drink remained the same, the surroundings evolved. Ever so slowly, reserved parlors and soda fountain scenes were superseded by casual surroundings. Women of good taste could now be found riding in a horse and buggy, playing tennis, or swimming at the beach. This 1897 vintage "Victorian Girl" Coca-Cola serving tray is the oldest of its kind known to exist—a graphic example of the demure themes used during the early Coca-Cola years. *Courtesy of The Coca-Cola Company*

"Bathing Beauty" serving tray, 1932

Below, center: In 1932, artist Hayden Hayden's work appeared on a Coca-Cola serving tray. The image chosen was nothing new and remained in line with the trays that came before it and those that came after: the thirsty bathing beauty. *Courtesy of The Coca-Cola Company*

"Have a Coke" serving tray, 1950–1952

Below, right: During World War II, North American girls waited patiently for their husbands and boyfriends to return home. In turn, the soldiers longed for jukeboxes, hamburgers, and sharing ice-cold Coca-Colas with their favorite gals. Those fortunate enough to receive curvy bottles in "care packages" from home became celebrities at the front, and an unopened Coca-Cola bottle was in such high demand that it could easily fetch $100! The worldwide market for Coca-Cola was unfolding. With the war's end, Coke was primed for its global debut. This Coca-Cola "pretty girl" serving tray was the first postwar model, a collectible frequently misdated as 1943 and 1948. *Courtesy of The Coca-Cola Company*

"The Coca-Cola Girl" serving tray, 1909

Above: The first tray issued by The Coca-Cola Company came out in 1909. Artist Hamilton King provided the "Coca-Cola Girl" image for the serving utensil, which was manufactured in Conshoctin, Ohio, by American Art Works, Inc. Well over one million repros of this example were turned out in the early 1970s. *Courtesy of The Coca-Cola Company*

Pepsi-Cola: A Nickel Drink That's Worth a Dime

Pepsi-Cola bottle, circa 1940
Above: After Charles Guth bought Pepsi-Cola in 1931, he decided to fix up the formula a bit, as he didn't care for the existing nuances in the drink's flavor. With haste, a sample syrup batch was sent to the lab, where chemist R. J. Ritchie fine-tuned the mixture. After a few weeks of tweaking, a new cola formula emerged. *Courtesy of the Pepsi-Cola Company*

"Healthful," 1910
Right: The early Pepsi-Cola metal trays from 1905 were mostly used to gather tips. Fashioned out of metal to mimic an earthenware delft design with blue lettering on a cream-colored field, these early trays advertised "The Pepsin Drink." Since the company changed hands so many times, few trays were manufactured overall. *Courtesy of the Pepsi-Cola Company*

Before the turn of the century, pharmacist Caleb Bradham's drugstore was a favorite gathering place for the residents of New Bern, North Carolina. In those days of horse-drawn carriages and gaslight, bottled soda refreshment was rare and soft drinks the domain of the neighborhood druggist. At Bradham's drugstore, his stomach-soothing concoction known as "Brad's Drink" became a favorite fountain mix, its taste energized by Bradham's addition of cola nut extract and pepsin, a digestive enzyme that breaks down protein.

By 1898, Bradham realized that a drink capable of calming the gut and refreshing the palate had a grand future. To instill the beverage with more universal appeal, he decided to rename it by combining the keystone ingredients into one catchy combination, Pepsi-Cola. To gain legal recognition, he filed a trademark application in 1902, and one year later, it was official.

Bradham organized the Pepsi-Cola Company and initiated the task of developing and marketing his drink to the masses. With luck his ally, he filled the corporate coffers by selling thousands of gallons of syrup within a few short months. By 1907, the demand became so great that the construction of a syrup and bottling plant was a necessity. As fortunes rose like so many carbonic bubbles, a three-story building was built to serve as the prestigious home office. By the time that Henry Ford's Model T was rolling off the assembly line in an endless stream, more than 280 franchised Pepsi-Cola bottlers were operating in twenty-four states.

But there was trouble brewing at the bottom of the bottle. As the United States entered World War I, the preeminent ingredient essential to the making of Bradham's syrup—sugar—began a roller-coaster price ride. Government controls temporarily held the price at 5½¢ a pound, but the laws of supply and demand quickly forced the cost skyward. In 1920, sugar was trading for 26¢ a pound, and it seemed people just couldn't get enough of it.

To hedge against further increases, Bradham made the mistake of his lifetime when he bought up large stocks of sugar at the exaggerated price. By December 1920, the cost of the crystalline commodity plummeted to the other end of the spectrum, bottoming out at below 2¢ a pound. As an unfortunate result, the Pepsi-Cola Company was in the red for $150,000 and never recovered.

Bradham eked by for two more years until forced to contact the Wall Street brokerage firm of R. C. Megargel & Company in hopes of salvaging the sinking company. Sadly, the reorganization plan was unsuccessful, and Pepsi-

"Pepsi-Cola Hits the Spot, Twelve Full Ounces, That's a Lot."—Pepsi slogan, 1930s

Cola was declared bankrupt in March 1923. One month later, Roy Megargel acquired the trademark and assets and formed the Pepsi-Cola Corporation as a Virginia company.

Mr. Megargel managed to maintain the company until the 1929 stock market crash, after which he found it increasingly difficult to continue funneling money into the firm. Eager to unload the floundering enterprise, he alerted New Yorker Charles Guth, then the president of Loft, Incorporated, to the impending bankruptcy. In 1931, the two men met in the Big Apple and agreed that Guth would finance the purchase of the Pepsi-Cola trademark, business, and goodwill. This third incarnation of pharmacist Caleb Bradham's dream would become a Delaware corporation known as the Pepsi-Cola Company.

The deal proved heaven sent, since fountain magnate Guth was currently at odds with his main syrup supplier, The Coca-Cola Company. At the time, Coke was being dispensed at all the fountains owned by Loft, including those operating under the "Mirror" and "Happiness" names. Because of the large syrup volume used at these soda bars, Guth felt he should receive a substantial discount on his flavoring purchases. Coca-Cola officials disagreed and remained stalwart in their policy of not selling directly to retailers. Loft was disallowed a discount, and the cola wars officially began.

Guth fired the first shot when he pulled Coca-Cola from Loft's two hundred fountain and candy stores in the New York metropolitan area and replaced it with his newly acquired Pepsi-Cola. Despite the fact that there was an immediate business drop, Guth calculated that it was only a matter of time before Pepsi gained its own following. Unlike previous cola beverages, Pepsi-Cola remained as the one and only trademark to survive the infringement litigation of The Coca-Cola Company. The trademark was a valuable commodity—one that was sure to spell eventual success for anyone who could see it through.

But Guth wasn't going to wait around for the public to get acquainted with the idea of a "pepsi" cola. While his stable of soda fountains provided an admirable cash flow for the Pepsi-Cola Company, there was a more expedient way to introduce the drink to the rest of America. In 1932, Guth came up with the idea to make a fancy, twelve-fluid ounce (360-ml) bottle that would sell exclusively at the Loft outlets for ten cents.

Unfortunately, initial sales reports were disappointing, and Guth began looking for a more influential inducement. He came to the conclusion that the depression-starved public could be easily enticed with a bargain. Instead of downsizing the bottle and reducing the price, he decided to sell the twelve-fluid ounce (360-ml) Pepsi for only five cents. "A nickel drink that's worth a dime" was a revolutionary idea for sales.

Guth knew that it wouldn't be long before other soft drink conglomerates copied his scheme, so he concentrated on building up high volume through generous franchise bottling initiatives. The strategy worked, and by 1936, the much heralded twelve-fluid ounce (360-ml) bottle was being filled by 313 American bottlers. At the end of the thirties, Pepsi-Cola was

"A bully drink," 1909
Above: In 1909, automobile racing pioneer Barney Oldfield became Pepsi's first celebrity endorser. As a national hero of the auto racing set, he appeared in newspaper ads of the age describing Pepsi-Cola as "A bully drink . . . refreshing, invigorating, a fine bracer before a race." The Coca-Cola slogan "delicious and healthful" came out that same year and would be used intermittently during the next two decades. *Courtesy of the Pepsi-Cola Company*

Horse-drawn Pepsi-Cola delivery wagon, circa 1910
In the early days, the Pepsi-Cola Company relied on good old-fashioned horse-drawn delivery wagons, just like everyone else. Here, a delivery team transports a load of bottles from Appalachia, Virginia. *Courtesy of the Pepsi-Cola Company*

occupying a sprawling manufacturing plant in Long Island City, New York. By then, the trademark script was registered in Canada, Cuba, and England, and the sweet, stomach-soothing flavor with added pepsin was taking a substantial market share away from Coke.

To its advantage, the Pepsi-Cola Company managed to keep the "Twice as Much for a Nickel" promotion going well into 1948. With a substantially cheaper price than Coca-Cola, a fabulous taste, and a visible foothold in the market, the zesty beverage ascended to the number two spot in the hierarchy of American colas.

"Pepsi and Pete" die-cut, circa 1940
Left, top: In 1931, the sudden switch from Coca-Cola to Pepsi at New York's Happiness and Loft fountains was viewed by many as a crime! With their favorite beverage barred from the soda fountain back bars, the response of New Yorkers was immediate: Fountain sales dropped from a high of thirty-one thousand gallons (117,800 liters) of syrup annually to a low of twenty-one thousand gallons (79,800 liters). In 1939, the newspaper comic strip "Pepsi and Pete" introduced the slogan "Twice as Much for a Nickel" to increase consumer awareness of Pepsi's value advantage. Pete was the little cop, Pepsi the big. *Courtesy of the Pepsi-Cola Company*

Pepsi comic strip ad, circa 1940s
Left, bottom: Jeepers, a rare example of a Pepsi-Cola color cartoon ad for all the kids who liked to cut a rug. *Author's Collection*

Jean Rogers and Bob Crosby, appearing in RKO Radio's "Let's Make Music."

WHEN THE STARS STEP OUT *Pepsi-Cola* IS A FAVORITE

Pepsi-Cola heads the order with those who order the best. Flavorful and fresh, Pepsi-Cola is welcomed by millions all over America. Feel your thirst disappear as that finer flavor hits the spot! Big help to any party—the big home carton of Pepsi-Cola—pick one up today.

A SPARKLING BEVERAGE
Pepsi-Cola
REFRESHING-SATISFYING
12 OUNCES

5¢
12 OZ. BOTTLE

"When the Stars Step Out . . .," 1941
Above: In 1941, Pepsi began a campaign featuring Hollywood stars and starlets. Appearing in RKO's *Let's Make Music*, Jean Rogers and Bob Crosby took time out to down a cold glass of Pepsi-Cola. The embossed, textured bottle is one of the most beautiful made by the company. *Author's Collection*

"Tempty . . . Tasty," circa 1941
Right: In support of America's war effort, Pepsi-Cola changed the color of its bottle crowns to red, white, and blue in 1941. A Pepsi canteen located in New York City's Times Square operated throughout the war years enabling more than a million families to record messages for armed service personnel overseas. *Preziosi Post-cards*

TEMPTY . . . TASTY
Pepsi-Cola

Chapter 4

Democracy in a Bottle

I'd like to build the world a home, and furnish it with love,
Grow apple trees and honey bees and snow-white turtle doves.
I'd like to teach the world to sing in perfect harmony,
I'd like to buy the world a Coke and keep it company.
Coca-Cola song, 1970s

Clean-cut days of drive-ins, tailfins, and Coke, 1959
Facing page: Back during the days of carhops and curb service, the Coca-Cola brand was synonymous with dining in your automobile. During the 1950s, car couples spent many an evening parked at the local eatery, dining on hamburgers, chomping on French fries, slurping down milkshakes, and sipping on ice-cold glasses of Coke. In those days of tailfins and convertibles, Styrofoam and paper cups were unheard of—only the distinctive bell-shaped Coca-Cola glasses were suitable for serving. *Author's Collection*

"Symbol of Friendship," circa 1960
Right: During the 1960s, the McKann Ericson ad agency debuted TV commercials that featured a chorus of young people gathered from around the globe, holding hands in a circle. Singing a universal song of Coke, "I'd Like to Teach the World to Sing," they suggested that anyone could access peace, love, harmony, and the good times just by buying a cold bottle of Coke. This "Symbol of Friendship" print ad was an early precursor to this idea of global soda serendipity. *Courtesy of The Coca-Cola Company*

Having survived the economic ravages of the Great Depression and two global wars, the carbonated trickle of soft drinks swelled into a raging river of effervescent exuberance. By the 1950s, the limited variety of flavors had flowed into a wide array of tastes. No longer fly-by-night concerns, bottling companies were braving the rapids. Now, they were responsible business entities—corporations with stockholders, research and development, national distribution channels, and advertising departments.

Symbol of Friendship

Companies had made great progress in making soft drinks a recognized part of the national scene. Still, there was one missing ingredient that had to be added before flavors like cola, ginger ale, lemon-lime, and root beer could saturate the taste buds of international pop culture. The problem was soda pop still retained its novelty status and was reserved for trips to the local soda fountain, picnics, or other special occasions. Buying a sweet bottle from a vending machine was a big deal too. Unlike today's soda-slamming practices, pop was idolized as a treat and not intended to wash down foods.

Pharmacy crew, 1932
Businesses like Friedman's Edgewood Pharmacy in Dallas, Texas, were bustling worlds of their own once upon a time, employing many of the workers that today labor under different roofs. The pharmacist, waitress, soda jerk, cleanup boy, and delivery driver—all were an integral part of Main Street marketing before the age of malls and strip centers robbed the soul of mom-and-pop enterprises. *Texas/Dallas History and Archives Division, Dallas Public Library*

Every once in a while, Mom might pick up a carton of bottles at one of the local supermarkets that were popping up on every corner—but even then, their consumption was regulated by strict rules and guidelines. Sis, Junior, and even Dad weren't allowed to fling open the Frigidaire door at will, pull out some chilled Cokes, pop the tops, and heartily drink away. Maybe a bottle could be shared at mealtime, but even then, the petite flasks didn't contain that much, and unbridled chugging was a definite no-no. As a result, milk, water, iced tea, and coffee reigned as the drinks of mealtime.

Naturally, this set of circumstances was of grave concern to the marketing gurus advising the major soft drink companies. Ever ready to expand the market and grow the industry, they began earnestly working to change consumer perceptions. Most importantly, take-home product had to be more accessible and easily carried. Retail prices had to be more affordable too. And as the rise of the post-World War II baby-boomer population threatened to shape the market, new flavors had to be considered.

As the prosperity of the fifties reached its zenith, car designers introduced new vehicles that embodied all the images of a hopeful future. At the same time, household appliance makers debuted the latest gadgetry. Homes became more efficient, and suburbia was hailed as the new model for living. Television was usurping the domain of radio, and before anyone could even object, the visual cues of styling rose to paramount importance. All at once, the naive ads born of yesteryear were outmoded. A new type of advertising was needed that touched drinkers where it mattered most—in their imaginations.

By consuming drink packaged with a particular brand or label, consumers were indirectly associating themselves with a variety of alter egos. Depending on brand, image-conscious imbibers pursed their lips for the libations that made them appear more sporty, sexy, racy, clever, subdued, humorous—and everything inbetween. To satisfy completely, soft drinks had to be comprised of more than just fizzing water, flavorings, and a nice label. For the consummate drinkers who desired more than simply great taste and color, soda pop had to create a fantasy that was accessible by the mere flick of a bottle opener.

Those Crazy Days of Carriages and Coca-Cola

During the early 1900s, this fantasy was well on its way toward becoming a tangible reality when an effort was undertaken to improve serving conditions at the soda fountains. At the time, the typical drugstore fountain was jammed in among pills, potions, and other sundries. At a counter positioned in front of the fountain, drinkers stood or seated themselves on stools; others took their refreshment at tables and chairs. All were part of an organized setting where men and women could interact with each other following the normal social conventions.

However, the cozy fountain setup wasn't free of problems: Women were regularly forced to mix with members of the opposite sex who they would rather have avoided. Consequently, a few of the more genteel patrons had to endure the disturbing habits of males and do their best to ignore the frequent spitting of chewing tobacco, fetid stench of cigar smoke, and off-color dialogue that was bandied about. It seemed that whenever a respectable mother took the time to escort her children to the local fountain for an invigorating round of bubbling sarsaparilla, there was always one loudmouth present who gained great pleasure from reciting the latest ribald tale or dirty limerick.

Fortunately, good things to come were introduced by a man of the same name, Harold Fortune. In 1905, he opened a drugstore in Memphis, Tennessee, and made himself a legend by pioneering a new technique for catering to the customers: carriage service. By all accounts, he enjoyed such a brisk soda fountain trade one hot summer that a few refined females refused to enter his establishment to get a drink. One male escort with exceptional manners struck upon the idea of having the ladies wait in their carriage while he ventured forth into the fountain area to order the catawba flips, sarsaparillas, and spa waters desired. After the drinks were in hand, he paid the bartender and delivered the refreshments to the gals waiting in their horse-drawn coach. Right there on the streetside, they drank.

By the end of the summer soda fountain season, the Memphis locals had all heard of this convenient in-carriage service, and pretty soon, they were all demanding it as a regular feature. Farmer Joe in his clapboard wagon and the local banker in his chauffeur-driven surrey were both vying for curbside space. Harold Fortune was cornered and responded in kind, directing the young men who were already tending to his counter area to take soda orders out to the street. As the task took up more time, a dedicated staff of delivery boys was hired to serve the increasing numbers lining up on the curb.

As would be expected, the radical method didn't remain a secret for long. The Coca-Cola Company, one of the leading producers of fountain syrup, took great notice of the trend and quickly incorporated the idea into their printed advertising pieces. Before long, full-color posters depicted fashionably dressed ladies perched high in their carriages while gracefully cradling a distinctive, bell-shaped glass of Coca-Cola. As sputtering gasoline-powered machines replaced the horse, the theme was modified to portray an automotive motif. The motorcar became the ultimate toy, and a new ad featured a motoring machine crammed full of passengers, all taking pleasure from glasses of soda.

By the time gas stations replaced livery stables, Fortune had moved his fountain to the Memphis business district to

Walgreen's soda fountain, circa 1940s
During the late 1920s, Walgreen Drugs was one of the Midwest's largest chain stores. Along with medicinal remedies and sundry merchandise, the soda fountain played a big part in the business. Geared to serving large quantities of soda beverages and ice cream treats, lunch counter soda jerks often served more than a hundred customers per hour. With a generous amount of whipped cream, syrup, and bubbling water, ice cream sodas were really fun to order from clean-cut lads like this one. *Hedrich-Blessing photograph/Chicago Historical Society*

Seven-Up collage

The Seven-Up flavor was introduced in 1928 by Charles Lieper Grigg of the Howdy Company, founded in 1920. The drink was originally named "Bib-Label Lithiated Lemon-Lime Soda," a title that was soon changed. Touted as the "cure for the common cola," mothers gave it to their children recovering from childhood illnesses like the flu. According to soda pop lore, Grigg came up with the 7UP moniker after spying a cattle brand of similar shape. He reckoned that if it was unique enough to identify cattle, it would stand out in the sale of soda. *Author/CoolStock*

serve the growing scores of commuters. With more cars being sold, a raft of automobilists soon made life miserable for all those just wishing to pass through town, and along the curb in front of Fortune's, the streets were always clogged with a line of cars waiting to stop in for a tumbler of cool carbonation. So Fortune broke away the curb and allowed cars to pull up on the sidewalk for service, but this solution didn't alleviate the problem. For nearby businesses, a law designed to ban all downtown curb service was the only remedy.

Soda Pop Becomes a Drive-In Staple

With his livelihood squelched by the new law, Fortune relocated his fountain setup to the outskirts of the city where he could conduct business the way he wished and serve as many cars as possible. By 1922, he had erected a totally new structure that featured an immense, separate fountain area, complete with a fully equipped kitchen and a parking/serving lot that many thought was way too big. In spite of the premature criticism, Fortune knew what he was doing—and what the public wanted. This was a soda stand where they could pull in, order a drink, and consume it in the privacy of their car.

Fortune was a year late when it came to inventing the concept that became known as the drive-in restaurant. In 1921, Dallas, Texas, tobacco magnate Jessie Kirby teamed up with physician Reuben Jackson to establish America's first dedicated drive-in drink-and-sandwich stand. From a tiny "Pig Stand" built on the Dallas–Fort Worth Highway, the pair introduced motorists to a barbecued entree of bread and meat called the Pig Sandwich.

Painted on large, pig-shaped signs, the slogan "Eat a Pig Sandwich" accompanied a pair of red-and-white placards that were posted on the building facade. The familiar, flowing script set in a field of crimson meant only one thing: Coca-Cola, the nation's most popular soft drink, was served.

Surprisingly, the icy cold bottles weren't delivered out to the car customers by the usual methods. As vehicles pulled in, young lads ran up to the arriving cars and jumped up onto the running boards—the thin strips beneath the doors then used as a step—to grab up the orders. Before the cars had even come to a complete stop, the boys were off running to the shack where they picked up the sandwiches and pop for delivery. Because they worked on tips alone, the serving activity was frenzied, almost manic. Shortly thereafter, this new, radical hybrid of waiter and showman was dubbed the carhop.

"People with cars are so lazy that they don't want to get out of them to eat!" were the words Kirby used when evangelizing the future investors who were interested in the unique dining arrangement. While his assumptions proved to be right, there was one small, important point that he had left out: To wash down all of that fast food barbecue that was being slung, the eclectic variety of patrons who were arriving in Fords, Chevrolets, and Cadillacs were also apt to down endless gallons of soda pop. Whether or not one called it eating, dining, or "the new motor lunch," it all required drink.

Meanwhile, other developments were taking place to cement the growing relationship of cars and carbonation. In California, Roy Allen was making a living ac-

"At the First Sign of Thirst," 1930s
The Roaring Twenties was a decade known for the prohibition of alcoholic beverages and the birth of the American institution known as the drive-in. The first dedicated drive-in restaurant was built in 1921 by Jessie Kirby and R. W. Jackson in Dallas, Texas, and called the Pig Stand. Savvy operators liked the format, copied it, and soon eating in the front seat of your car was an all-out national craze. By the end of the 1920s, curb stands were everywhere, and soft drinks like Dr Pepper were accepted as the perfect companion for hand-held foods. Bottlers exploited the culinary union in any way they could, utilizing ads to carry forth the tasty message. *Courtesy of the Dr Pepper Museum, Waco, Texas*

"2-4-6-8 . . . What Do We Appreciate?," 1958
During the late 1950s, Seven-Up marketed to the easy-going carhop crowd with color advertising printed in major periodicals. Like many of the other soda pop makers, it discovered that there wasn't anything more powerful than the combination of attractive young people having a good time, a jaunty roadster, and a visit to the local drive-in diner. *Author's Collection*

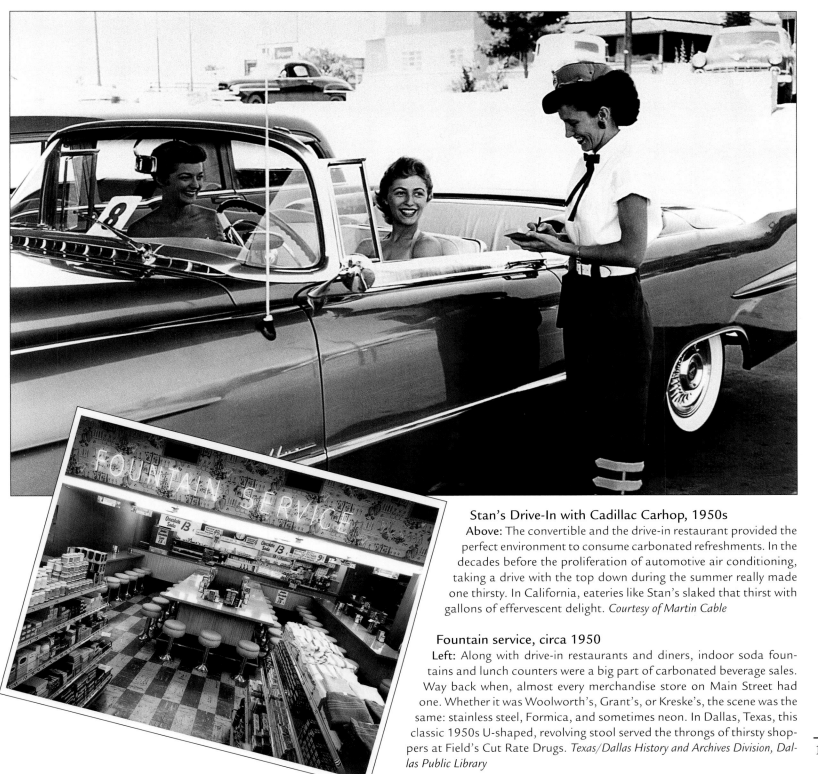

Stan's Drive-In with Cadillac Carhop, 1950s

Above: The convertible and the drive-in restaurant provided the perfect environment to consume carbonated refreshments. In the decades before the proliferation of automotive air conditioning, taking a drive with the top down during the summer really made one thirsty. In California, eateries like Stan's slaked that thirst with gallons of effervescent delight. *Courtesy of Martin Cable*

Fountain service, circa 1950

Left: Along with drive-in restaurants and diners, indoor soda fountains and lunch counters were a big part of carbonated beverage sales. Way back when, almost every merchandise store on Main Street had one. Whether it was Woolworth's, Grant's, or Kreske's, the scene was the same: stainless steel, Formica, and sometimes neon. In Dallas, Texas, this classic 1950s U-shaped, revolving stool served the throngs of thirsty shoppers at Field's Cut Rate Drugs. *Texas/Dallas History and Archives Division, Dallas Public Library*

quiring hotel properties, refurbishing them, and then reselling them for a tidy profit. While checking over a property for sale in Flagstaff, Arizona, he met a traveling chemist who raved about a wonderful formula he had concocted for a frothy, exceedingly tasty draft root beer. The chemist promised that with his formula and Allen's backing, the drink could be sold in mugs at a nickel a glass, and within a short time, a fortune could be made.

After Allen sampled a taste, he agreed to join forces with the inventor to manufacture and market the root beer concentrate to the general public. Allen wasted little time opening a tiny root beer refreshment stand in the city of Lodi, California. The concession was situated on a busy street corner in the downtown area and proved to be an ideal location to peddle icy drinks. It was 1919 and Prohibition was in full swing. As a result, public demand for the secret root beer mixture of herbs, spices, barks, and berries swelled to great proportions.

Since the modest root beer stand was showing a respectable profit, Allen decided to open a similar stand in the nearby town of Stockton. In 1920, employee Frank Wright (who started at the original Lodi location) threw in his lot with Allen, and the search for a new business name began. Opting for simplicity, the pair chose the first letters of their last names, "A" for Allen, and "W" for Wright. The foaming root beer that promised to increase their fortunes would now be called A & W Root Beer.

On a bustling corner of K and Nineteenth Streets in nearby Sacramento, Allen and Wright opened their first A & W Root Beer stand in 1921. Like the Texas Pig Stand, their service would be based on the concept of bringing the orders to the cars. At first, they enrolled the services of young men called tray boys to carry out the drinks; later, they hired an attractive bevy of tray girls to serve. After two years, there were three A & W stands doing business in town and seemingly no end to their popularity in sight.

Despite the success, Wright later disposed of his interest in the company, and Allen forged ahead alone. Using the same A & W name, he began an aggressive expansion campaign and managed to propel the trio of orange-and-black root beer stands toward national presence by selling franchises in the American West and Midwest. By 1933, the letters A & W had become a familiar sight to those travelers in search of cold refreshment. By then, 171 of the stands in various shapes and sizes marked the American roadways.

Inspired by the success of Allen's root beer shacks, others attempted to reap the fortunes of soda pop, and soon a wave of roadside hot dog stands, diners, greasy spoons, and cafes opened for business. As the roadsides filled up with food stops from coast to coast, the marriage of cars and colas became an official union. Signs selling soda pop became a regular sight— hung on trees, plastered onto buildings, planted in vacant lots, and wherever the eye (and the thirst centers of the brain) could see them. Available anywhere and anytime, soda pop had become a ubiquitous commodity.

Repackaging the Magic for Convenience

In order to make carbonated soft drinks as commonplace in the home as they were along the road, the American beverage industry adopted the carry-home carton for widespread use in 1928. Within a decade, it proved a marketing marvel that resulted in sales of 70 million cartons per year. Harried homemakers learned of the hand-held convenience by way of a national ad blitz, and shortly thereafter, they headed straight to their local grocery stores to pick up a few packs. The new method of merchandising soda pop became so popular that, by 1957, sales of the six-bottle cartons exceeded 700 million units per year.

Unfortunately, there was one major problem with the empty bottles once they were drained of their drink: Customers always returned them to the point of purchase so that they could get their deposit back. As the returns stacked up, merchants were forced to store empties until they could be transported back to their respective bottlers. Soft drink companies had to pay shippers to retrieve the used containers. When they were finally returned to the place whence they came, there was still more work to be done: Dirty bottles had to be cleaned, disinfected, and inspected before they could be refilled and resold.

In 1931, Canada Dry made the first effort to eliminate these practices when it debuted the first non-returnable soda pop bottle. Unfortunately, the new, lightweight grade of glass that was specified for the containers added additional costs that had to be passed on to consumers. Other manufacturers decided that switching to the new method was too great a marketing risk, and with that, an idea that was years ahead of its time lost support within the bottling industry. But the answer was out there, and the major players continued the search for a cheap, easy-to-manufacture throwaway.

Since metal was cheaper than glass, thoughts turned to using tin for soda containers. In 1936, Clicquot Club with its mascot the smiling Eskimo lad became the first soft drink manufacturer to experiment with the use of metal when it introduced an unusual can with a cone top (later, refiners used a similar container to package motor oil). Ironically, the existing technology didn't allow manufacturers to produce a technically superior seal for contents that were under pressure. The acidulants in fruit flavorings were reacting to the metal and spoiling the taste too. Since the problems could never be satisfactorily addressed, the project was abandoned. When World War II started, the quest for cans was put on hold.

After the war, the concerted effort to perfect and manufacture the tin can as an acceptable one-way delivery system was renewed. Soda pop producers were ready to move beyond the glass bottles, since cans made of metal promised new advantages. With relative ease, tin containers could be imprinted with bright colors and graphics. Furthermore, they offered a significant weight savings over glass, even when they were full of pop. But most important, they only traveled one way to where they would be sold. Truly "no deposit, no return," they eliminated the age-old problem of refurbishing bottles.

When the dilemma of leaky seams was finally solved, designers realized that a practical method to release the contents from a can had yet to be devised. The solution came in the form of a "church key," a special can opener that had to be used by customers in order to puncture the

Dallas pharmacy carhop, circa 1925
In 1925, when car customers were just beginning to get a taste of what car dining was all about, male "runners" were a visible part of the pharmacy equation. Busy pharmacies like the Highland Park in Dallas, Texas, first employed soda jerks inside the store and hired delivery boys to carry out ice cream and sodas to vehicles queued at the curb. The job requirements: fleetness of foot, a good sense of balance (to carry two trays stacked with drinks), and a willingness to serve the public with style and grace. *Texas/Dallas History and Archives Division, Dallas Public Library*

Prohibition raid, 1920s
A police raid conducted by law officers in Dallas, Texas, during the prohibition days of the Roaring Twenties uncovered a trove of illegal booze. While the many patrons of underground bars, or speakeasies, guzzled down alcohol, the rest of the United States was trying to get by without distilled spirits. The only drinks left that could wet one's whistle were soda pop and ice cream concoctions. *Texas/Dallas History and Archives Division, Dallas Public Library*

held shoot-'em-up slingshot contests. The space age had arrived in the form of a thin-walled aluminum container that exhibited the same properties as tin without the bulk.

Despite its superiority, the aluminum can was cursed with one distressing design feature that wasn't universally accepted. Some aficionados heralded it as the flip-top, a few called it the pull-tab, while others just cursed it as litter. When torn away from the body of the can, the handy tab that revealed a triangular drinking hole became an instant piece of garbage. Regrettably, there wasn't a practical way to store the nasty cast-off until the drink was done. The pleasure of going barefoot during summer was over as evidence of the aluminum can's success was scattered about on streets, sidewalks, and beaches.

Just about the time that the paper soda bottle label slipped into the annals of ancient history, the menace of the aluminum can pull-tab was remedied. In the same spirit as the vanguards who shook up the bottling world during the 1900s, one enterprising inventor solved the problem of the pesky pull-top. Now, instead of pulling the opening off of the can and then tossing it to the wind, a built-in "can-opener" could be pulled up by one carefully placed finger. A quick jerk pushed a pre-punched opening down into the can. The tab remained attached and was held there until the entire unit could be recycled.

Spreading the Gospel of Carbonation

And so, the saga of the soda can continued into the 1990s, when soda makers introduced all sorts of packaging innova-

metal disk that formed the top of the container. Not one, but two openings were required: One of the triangular holes was used to pour out the pop while the other equalized the pressure so that the contents could flow out steadily. After one big chug-a-lug of drink, the tin can was thrown into the trash, never to be used again.

But even though the mighty tin can had finally achieved its ultimate configuration, it wasn't immune to replacement. By 1958, it lost its position in the hierarchy of soda pop containers when an economical can crafted of lightweight aluminum was produced. Within a few years, the tin can's reputation for strength was superseded. Gone were the days when children donned crushed-can shoes, played crush-the-can strongman, and

tions. Among the most unusual, the Virgin Cola label unveiled a glass bottle in the shape of a woman with a picture of buxom *Baywatch* TV show star Pamela Anderson Lee adorning the label. Of course, Coca-Cola was not to be outclassed. In 1996, the soft drink corporation unwrapped their own line of curvaceous beauties when a bold plan was announced to introduce new aluminum containers that would be modeled after their signature contoured bottles.

To other competitors in the worldwide soda industry, the bold move to redefine the shape of the standard soft drink can came as no great surprise. Long before the turn of the century, when the idea of bringing soda waters to the public was still a relatively fresh one, Coca-Cola pioneers Asa Candler and Frank Robinson were already setting the pace for their contemporaries. But back in those days, soda bottles were still regarded as utilitarian objects. Because of technical considerations, they varied little in design. Other, more flamboyant methods were employed to recruit new customers to drink cola.

To the pair's good credit, this need for advertising didn't result in visual banality. By no means. They sought out a stable of talented artists and painters to create some of America's most remembered advertising scenes. Throughout the 1880s and 1890s, Candler and Robinson hired commercial lithographers to print color posters of these intricate, decorative artworks. But instead of languishing in the confines of a dusty museum, the colorful Coca-Cola imprints were distributed to all participating drugstores, soda fountains, and syrup dealers for public display.

When four-color printing became practical, Atlanta's Massengale advertising agency was hired to transfer the masterpieces onto the pages of popular magazines. Although the medium was smaller, the visual composition of the advertising remained the same: Posed in opulent settings, fashionable ladies and gentlemen dressed in elegant attire sipped from tumblers of Coca-Cola. The inference? Anyone who had the wherewithal to hand over a nickel for a glass had instant access to the good life.

During this formative period of innocuous motifs, Coca-Cola employed a vigorous program of dealer incentives as well. Although not a direct pitch to the consumer, it motivated retailers to sell more sodas and allowed the general public to familiarize themselves with the brand name. The scheme was simple enough: According to the volume of syrup moved by the soda fountain proprietors, a variety of bonus items were bestowed upon them, some imprinted with the Coca-Cola trademark. A few of these sales awards were quite decorative and included Baird clocks, porcelain fountain urns, prescription scales, and merchandise display cases.

After 1920, the initial amazement over artificially carbonated water began to decline, and the marketing focus changed. The middle class was growing, and society was adopting new social values. So, Coca-Cola and its many imitators changed with the times to become democracy in a bottle, a great common denominator of drink that endeavored to cut across all social and economic boundaries. None too soon, the over-embellished Victorian scenes of the founding days were phased out to make way for

Coca-Cola cooler at gas pump island, circa 1928
In 1928, the first Coca-Cola chest coolers were a big hit with retail proprietors. At general stores and filling stations across the land, basic models produced by the Glasscock Brothers Manufacturing Company became permanent fixtures to serve the modern motorist. Unlike today's refrigerated dispensing machines, these simple bottle bins utilized cracked ice that was delivered by another vestige of a forgotten era, the ice man. *Courtesy of The Coca-Cola Company*

A & W Root Beer stand, circa 1925
Above: "Tray-boys" and "tray-girls" provided the outside service at early A & W Root Beer stands like this one in Salt Lake City, Utah. Hustling trays laden down with frosty mugs of the brew, they rushed between arriving cars to take orders and satisfy the public's thirst. *Courtesy of A & W Restaurants, Inc.*

A & W Root Beer stand, circa 1930s
Right: Although Prohibition was repealed in 1933, A & W Root Beer stands like this one continued to thrive. Despite the national love for liquor and the ceaseless yen for brewed beer containing alcohol, there was always the desire for an occasional root beer float. *Courtesy of A & W Restaurants, Inc.*

A & W Root Beer stand, 1933

A & W Root Beer grew in popularity in the 1920s after Roy Allen and Frank Wright teamed to market the flavorful brew. The duo's first stand was located in Lodi, California, and was soon joined by others nationwide. Many of these early structures played with fantastic, programmatic architecture and relied on the theme of the building structure to pull in the customers, as with this stand in South Bend, Indiana. To attract the motorists passing by, what could be more appropriate than a giant root beer barrel? *Courtesy of A & W Restaurants, Inc./CoolStock*

A & W mugs on a car tray, 1990s

Drive-in service was the backbone of the A & W restaurants from their inception in the 1920s until their exodus to the strip malls in the 1970s. While it's enjoyable to sip a cold flagon of sweet brew while sitting in an air-conditioned food court, there is nothing like downing a frothy, icy mug while seated in the front seat of the family automobile. *Author*

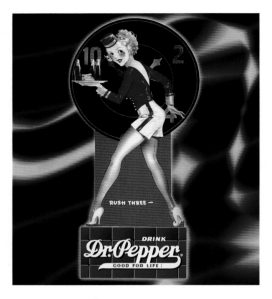

Dr Pepper carhop, 1940s
In the heyday of tray food from the 1920s until the late 1960s, the car server known as the carhop was the queen of the American drive-in. Part social director, part showgirl, and part waitress (or waiter if the carhop was male), she strutted her stuff with particular pluck and sass. Her task was an important one, and she knew it. Stacked with all the delights that any red-blooded American car customer could desire, she served her way into history—proudly holding her tray high and flashing her come-hither smile for all to see. Brands like Dr Pepper capitalized on the sexy image to sell soda and used point-of-purchase display cutouts like this countertop model to move gallons of carbonated delights. *Courtesy of the Dr Pepper Museum, Waco, Texas*

more accessible settings. The new idea was to utilize familiar patriotic images and identify the soda beverage with the nation itself. When the thirsty consumer thought of America, a waving flag of soda pop was to be one of the central images that played over in the theater of the mind.

Even when the Great Depression of the 1930s dampened spirits, Coca-Cola marketing chose to ignore the negativity and popularized a soothing new slogan. In ads that touted "The Pause That Refreshes," carefree soda sippers consumed cola as they traveled the world, enjoying all the luxuries that airplane, train, and car travel had to offer. In 1931, the Christmas holidays were made even more bubbly when artist Haddon Sundblom's rosy-cheeked Santa Claus was seen polishing off a bottle of Coke on billboards nationwide. Even old St. Nick was pausing from his work for refreshment.

There were even more happy images to come: Shapely girls in bathing suits thrust out icy bottles for the public's approval, as did famous movie stars, admired sports celebrities, and other great figures of conspicuous notoriety. Definitely in were scenes that conjured up positive thoughts and warm, fuzzy feelings such as those evoked by Norman Rockwell paintings that graced the cover of the *Saturday Evening Post*. Soda pop was to remain a "feel-good thing" without any discord or controversy.

Putting the Pop in Popular Culture

The age of innocence did not last forever. By the fifties, television changed the direction of advertising, and the prized painted images were dropped in favor of bold, colorful graphics. Coca-Cola ads shunned the images that showcased people in fun situations doing fun things. Suddenly, all the human elements were dropped; inanimate objects became the main focus.

Strange as it seemed, the new rationale was somewhat logical: Art directors came to the conclusion that neutral items like a tennis racket, golf clubs, or a plate of food would not offend those with hang-ups—prejudices would be a more appropriate term—as pictures of real people could. Instead of depicting a diverse range of soda-drinking participants and showing them partaking of the beverage in different versions of an advertisement, it was deemed more prudent to provide the public with a generic scene that anyone could place themselves in.

The impersonal ad trend eventually reversed itself, and by 1968, diverse groups were once again acknowledged. That year, the McKann Ericson ad agency chose to recognize the existence of hippies in a humorous, two-page Coke ad. As the war in Vietnam raged, the ad firm pushed the envelope even further with the debut of a commercial featuring a chorus of young people from all nations, holding hands. Singing a universal song of Coke, "I'd Like To Teach The World To Sing," they reintroduced the soft drink's original message to all those that wanted to hear it: Coca-Cola was a product that anyone could use to access peace, love, harmony, and the good times. It truly was "The Real Thing."

By the mid-1990s, the advertising machine that was started up so long ago had achieved its ultimate goal. The carbonic beverage had become such an integral part of the world's collective consciousness that it finally replaced water as the drink of choice. Men, women, children, seniors—it seemed that everyone was downing soda pop on any occasion. People could no longer live without it, and besides, nobody really wanted to. Although it was surely a gimmick to foster brand recognition, grocery stores were even stocking up on minuscule baby bottles that were imprinted with familiar beverage brands. Soda pop had at long last become the default drink, consumed from the cradle to grave.

A symbol of this devotion arrived on April 23, 1985, when The Coca-Cola Company changed its time-tested formula and introduced New Coke with a sweeter taste that some compared to Pepsi. Worshipful customers loyal to the original blend bombarded the firm with emotional pleas to bring back the original formula, and the company's toll-free phone number was jammed with complaints. Ten weeks later, Coca-Cola complied to the backlash and brought back the favorite icon under the name Coca-Cola Classic. At the same time, it held onto the new formula—but New Coke didn't survive long, and eventually only the original formula remained.

There were many good reasons for the devotion. Ads suggested that just by downing a cold can of pop, ordinary people could readily tap into the elements of personality that they lacked. Anyone could retain their individuality yet join the club and "Be a Pepper too." If one chose to "Do The Dew," he or she gained entry to the counterculture world of bungee-jumpers. Minding calories became a secondary concern and drinking a diet Coke was done "Just for the Taste of It." When the new generation wasn't chortling down a Pepsi, they were at-

Triple XXX Thirst Station, 1949
More than fifty years ago, before there were any McDonalds, Burger Kings, and Wendys, mom-and-pop drive-ins like Bill Wood's Triple XXX Root Beer Stand served up the bulk of America's soda drinks. Located on the infamous traffic "Circle" in Waco, Texas, Wood's famous stand is now a memory. *Author's Collection*

tempting to bring out the "Sprite in You" with a lemon-lime drink.

Soda pop had definitely come full circle. From its early days as patent medicine, through its golden years as a treat, to its final rise to become a part of pop culture, it was here to stay. Although it was no longer a medicine for the ailing body, it had evolved into a complete tonic for the mind and the soul.

Soda pop patches

While today's beverage delivery personnel may still be identified by the brand of patch affixed to their uniforms, the roster of visible brands has dwindled. The year 1929 was the biggest for bottling plants with 7,920 in the United States alone; by 1949, there were 6,907; by 1986, there were but 1,380. In Canada, there were more than 500 independent soft drink bottlers by 1942 in addition to the numerous franchise company-owned bottling plants; by 1956, there were 535 bottlers operating in 258 communities. This collage of surviving and long-defunct labels is a tribute to the colorful flavors that once enriched the rainbow of soda pop. *Author*

Whistling for Whistle, circa 1920

Right: In 1919, Charles Lieper Grigg worked for a St. Louis, Missouri, manufacturing firm owned by Vess Jones. Grigg was the firm's top salesman and came up with a new orange drink he called Whistle. Imprinted with the slogan, "It's cloudy in the bottle," Whistle rose to become the company's top seller. As a result, Grigg was promoted and assumed the number two post at the company. However, problems arose between him and Vess, causing Grigg to find his fame and fortune elsewhere. In 1928, he debuted a new lemon-lime drink that became Seven-Up. *Author's Collection*

"Lawful Larceny," *The Saturday Evening Post*, 1926

Facing page: In 1926, Orange-Crush promoted "lawful larceny" to mothers across the United States. The message: What could be more nourishing for kids than a bottle of orange soda? After all, it was a true fruit-flavored drink with "real food value!" The Orange-Crush Company was founded by California chemist N. C. Ward, who joined with soft-drink merchandiser C. J. Howell in Chicago and opened the first Orange-Crush plant in 1916. Contrary to the older processes that used orange extract, he developed a way to mechanically break up the oils of an orange and then suspend them in an emulsion. These so-called "cloudy orange" drinks were all the rage during the mid-1910s, despite the fact that consumers had to shake them before drinking. *Author's Collection*

The kids are on!

Sure as Sam Hill, the kids do like to "Whistle".

And grown-ups say it's liquid happiness in bottles.

You'll say so, too! Look around and you'll see a place to

WHISTLE

"Lawful Larceny"

MOTHERS—you can safely give the children all the Orange-Crush they like. For Orange-Crush is a true fruit-flavored drink, has real food value. To healthful carbonated water is added the juice of luscious oranges—the delicate flavor of their peel—the zestful tang of the fruit acid found in oranges, lemons and limes—a pure food color, such as you use in your cakes and candies—pure cane sugar.

Keep Orange-Crush always on ice. Serve it at meals.—A delightfully refreshing drink.

Ward's Orange-CRUSH

We just canned our top salesman.

Canada Dry ad with early can, 1960s
Above, left: By the end of the 1960s, most major bottlers in North America switched to the metal can. Canada Dry responded to consumer demand for more durable packaging and unveiled this ad in magazines. Its new slogan: "Canada Dry beverages always were unbeatable. Now they're unbreakable, too." *Author's Collection*

Dr Pepper cans, circa 1954
Above, right: In 1936, Clicquot Club was the first to use metal for packaging when it introduced the cone-top can. Other bottlers followed its lead and later incorporated a refined version of the design to package their own products. This trio of containers were non-returnable types adopted by Dr Pepper in 1954. Three sizes were made available to a test market in St. Louis, Missouri: a 6½- and 10-ounce (195- and 300-ml) cone top, and a 12-ounce (360-ml) regular-style can. *Author/Dr Pepper Bottling Company of Dublin*

Experimental Coca-Cola can, circa 1960s
Right: Coca-Cola was not left out in the exodus to the tin can. Although its products would still remain in distinctive glass bottles of various sizes during the years to come, the can became a great means to promote the drink to a public with more recreation and leisure time. On the beach, at the park, or while camping, the soda can was king during the 1960s. *Courtesy of The Coca-Cola Company*

"It's Cott to Be Good!" postcard, circa 1930s

Left: The Cott Corporation was originally based in New Haven, Connecticut, and in the early 1950s, Cott beverage products were exported to Canada. By 1955, Cott incorporated and began bottling its own products in Quebec. In 1962, Cott purchased Clicquot Club and added the bottling facilities in Millis, Massachusetts. In 1981, the Cott trademark was acquired by Canada Dry. Cott ceased bottling and began packaging private brands for Canadian grocery-store chains. *Preziosi Postcards*

Matchbooks montage

Above: As a free giveaway item handed out in restaurants, businesses, bus terminals, and other public places, the matchbook was once a great advertising medium. Soda bottlers recognized the marketing potential of the tiny billboards and earnestly used them to promote their brands. Now that most examples are a scarce commodity, philluminists (matchbook collectors) gather them for posterity. *Author/CoolStock*

Dr Pepper syrup jugs, 1930s to 1960s
Right: Before the era of plastics changed the way fluids are stored, Dr Pepper syrup for vending and fountains was shipped to retailers in large glass jugs. At the earliest soda fountains, the jugs were inverted and then cradled in an elevated holder that dispensed the syrup from below. In a second step, the carbonated water was added from another spigot. By the 1940s, improved dispensers integrated both the soda water and syrup outlets into a single unit. With the pull of one lever, the soda jerk filled single cups with ease. *Author/Dr Pepper Bottling Company of Dublin*

Coca-Cola for export, 1930s
Bottom, left: During the late 1920s and early 1930s, Coca-Cola made a great effort to market its famous soft drink overseas. The marketing expertise of the Foreign Department, later called The Coca-Cola Export Corporation, provided the means to get the drink better known in Europe. As part of the program, a special package known as the Export Bottle was designed for the foreign markets and used exclusively on ocean liners. This handsome, labeled bottle looked like it contained much more than a mere soda beverage and caused many overseas operators to inquire about the possibility of bottling it. *Courtesy of The Coca-Cola Company*

Dr Pepper 10-2-4 thermometer, 1930s
Bottom, right: To differentiate its script lettering from Coca-Cola's, Dr Pepper changed the red background in 1934. At the time, the Samuel Stamping & Enameling Company in Georgia was soliciting the company to make metal signs for its coolers. It asked for pounce patterns so that the signs would be accurately reproduced. As the story goes, the Dr Pepper ad department supplied patterns that had lined squares behind the logo; this grid was intended only as an accuracy scale to be used in reproduction. Six weeks later, the sign maker sent samples of its offering to Dr Pepper, and to the firm's amazement, the grid squares were part of the logo! Officials were amused—but liked it. They decided to use the new design. *Author/Dr Pepper Museum, Waco, Texas*

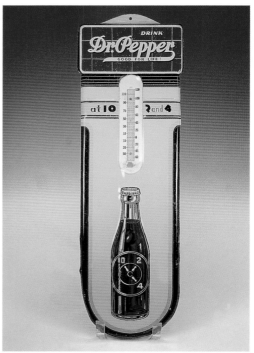

Crossroads store, circa 1930s
During the Great Depression, soda pop was just one of those commodities that was difficult to live without. Made of wood, metal, or clad in porcelain enamel, signs were plastered along the byways, sometimes obliterating the structures they were fastened upon. Radio was only beginning to hold its own as an advertising medium, and television didn't exist. Major brands relied on the painted billboard to sell their sodas, and as a consequence, signs were nailed up wherever empty space was found. *Library of Congress*

Dr Pepper neon clock
Columbia University research in the 1920s showed that the hours of 10, 2, and 4 were the precise times that an average person's energy level diminished. Capitalizing on this finding, Dr Pepper debuted the slogan "Drink a Bite to Eat at 10, 2, and 4 o'clock" in 1926. As fate would have it, the admonition became Dr Pepper's most successful advertising slogan! There was good reason: Dr Pepper was packed with inverted sugars that were quickly absorbed into the bloodstream. Downing a cold bottle or two produced an instantaneous energy lift that worked to prevent this daily cycle of fatigue. Customers bought the concept, and the phrase remained an integral part of the brand's packaging for decades. *Courtesy of the Dr Pepper Museum, Waco, Texas*

Mission Orange patriotic gal, circa early 1940s
Right: Mission Orange emerged during the early 1930s to a market receptive to orange-flavored drinks. This vintage "Everybody's Choice" postcard made good use of the patriotic fervor that was sweeping the United States during World War II. *Preziosi Postcards*

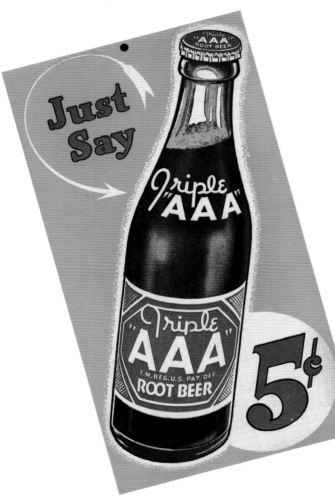

"Just Say Triple AAA" cardboard sign, 1946
Above: The Triple AAA Company of Oklahoma City, Oklahoma, produced one of the competitors to Hires and A & W. Believe it or not, today's popular root beer soft drinks were born of the beer-making skills developed by North America's English settlers. Once mixed up by the homemaker, these non-alcoholic beers were tasty beverages for the whole family to enjoy. *Author's Collection*

Betty Grable for Royal Crown, 1940s

Left: Beginning in 1941, well-known Hollywood stars and starlets were featured in national magazine ads for RC. Pin-up girl Betty Grable was one of the most memorable celebrities, with her million-dollar legs—insured, of course—and unforgettable smile vying for attention with the ad copy. Betty preferred Royal Crown when she tried it in a blind taste test. Royal Crown had pioneered the "taste test" during the 1940s and conducted them in public places like hotel lobbies and train terminals. *Author's Collection*

Our Gang votes for Royal Crown, 1941

Right: To battle the aggressive marketing of Coca-Cola, competitors looked for any advantage they could get: The Nehi Corporation used the familiar faces of the *Our Gang* comedy series to get the word out on Royal Crown Cola, and Spanky, Buckwheat, Froggy, and the rest of the gang all reached for a bottle of RC. Nehi's president after 1933, Hilary Richard Mott, first came up with the idea for the cola drink in 1934. It was packaged in a twelve-ounce (360-ml) bottle and became the second cola after Pepsi-Cola to compete with the industry leader, the six-ounce (180-ml) bottle of Coca-Cola. *Author's Collection*

FOR HAPPY HOLIDAYS AT HOME!

The All-Family Drink!

So pure... So good... So wholesome for everyone!

7up

REG. U.S. PAT. OFF.

You like it... it likes you!

Drink A BITE TO EAT at 10 2 4

DRINK
Dr. Pepper
GOOD FOR LIFE!

Santa and his sleigh ad, 1949
Above: Like Coca-Cola, Dr Pepper, and a host of other flavors, Seven-Up jumped on the holiday sleigh with Santa Claus ads geared at selling its own brand. This whimsical portrayal of old St. Nick made it clear that receiving a bottle of the Uncola was on the same level as getting a gift. *Author's Collection*

Parachuting Santa, 1940s
Right: The parachuting Santa Claus cutout was given to dealers to hang and display. The man in the red suit was a potent image for marketing pop, and many brands employed the North Pole resident as salesman. This example was probably conceived during the war years when paratroopers were jumping into enemy territory. *Courtesy of the Dr Pepper Museum, Waco, Texas*

Santa Claus and Coke montage

Santa Claus has appeared on a variety of Coca-Cola ads since 1930. The image of St. Nicholas, the patron saint of children from Asia Minor (circa A.D. 300), was reshaped in 1844 when poet Clement Clark Moore published "'Twas the Night Before Christmas." Describing Santa as a "plump, jolly old elf," Moore's work influenced artists for the next fifty years, causing them to paint Santa Claus as a gnomelike creature! By 1900, confusion reigned as Christmas cards imported from Europe didn't adhere to Moore's imagery. The only constant was a white beard, Christmas tree, and toys. In 1930, Coca-Cola printed a magazine ad with a realistic, human-sized version of the benevolent gift-giver, people responded favorably, and the ad became a regular feature. In 1931, artist Haddon Sundblom began working for Coca-Cola and set upon the task of focusing the Santa image. Retired Coke salesman Lou Prentice was used as the model for years, and later, when he passed away, Sundblom used his own face! The result became the rotund, happy, red-suited, white-bearded, black-booted, North Pole stereotype we know and love as Santa Claus today. *Courtesy of The Coca-Cola Company/ CoolStock*

Nehi Six Pack coupon, circa 1950s
Claude Adkin Hatcher debuted a new line of fruit drinks under the name Nehi in 1924. The idea for the brand originated after a local sales manager Felix Patrick, Sr. told Hatcher: "I saw a soda in Phenix City today that was knee high!" Using risqué advertising signs that featured a "glamorous leg" and posting them far and wide, the flavorful new soda drinks quickly gained a fervent following. Nehi began as Union Bottling Works in 1905 in Columbus, Georgia, changing its name to Chero-Cola in 1912, to Nehi in 1928, and finally to Royal Crown Cola Company in 1959. *Author's Collection*

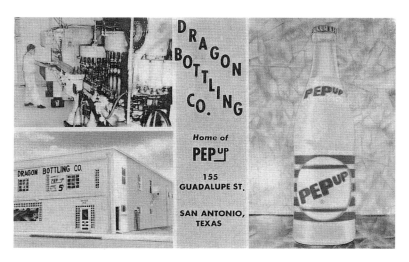

"Home of Pep Up" postcard, circa 1950s
The Dragon Bottling Company was established as a wholesale beverage manufacturer in 1915. Once located in San Antonio, Texas, it was famous for its Dragon Beverage and a drink called Pep Up, proclaimed as the "largest soda water for a nickel." *Preziosi Postcards*

"Get Chummy with Rummy" ad, 1948
Made from the juice of golden, ripe grapefruit, Rummy was one company's answer to the snappy citrus beverage in 1948. Produced by the Wonder-Orange Company of Chicago, Illinois, this all-juice, non-alcoholic drink enjoyed a rather short life on the grocer's shelf. While the slogan was somewhat catchy, there was little doubt that the name conjured up images of winos and drunkenness—not the perfect image for selling pop! *Author's Collection*

The Silent Salesmen of Soda Pop

*We have a special place in our hearts
for these soda machines, because like the
cars and the jukeboxes, we continue to want
them in our lives after their practicality
has expired.*
Jeff Walters, *Classic Soda Machines*

At the turn of the century, the methods for pmarketing soft drinks were confined to the retail environment. To enhance their soda sales, merchants utilized whatever materials were on hand. As a result, wooden barrels, steel washtubs, and even buckets provided point-of-purchase display for bottles of pop.

Back then, bulk "refrigerant" was delivered by the local iceman in the form of a frozen block of ice to be crushed and spread atop the glass containers to keep them cool. To make a selection, thirsty customers thrust their hands into the frigid soup, pulled out their favorite flavor, and paid the proprietor.

To heighten the visual awareness of product, a few pioneering merchants improvised by sawing the wooden barrels in half and turning the pieces on their ends. Legs were attached to the two halves of the casks, creating a pair of waist-level merchandising stations that could be readily placed in front of the store or near the cash register. To identify the sweet brand being sold, shopkeepers nailed pressed-tin and porcelain-enameled advertising signs provided by bottlers to the front of these bins.

While the impromptu sales arrangement appeared satisfactory for selling beverages, there was room for improvement. Clerks who were spending too much time making change and small talk realized that their time would be better served if customers helped themselves. If patrons could purchase a bottle of pop without assistance, all the better. A self-contained, mechanical vending machine that combined the properties of a storage cabinet, drink cooler, and coin collector was the ultimate solution.

By the mid-twenties, a variety of specialized coolers appeared on the market to satisfy this need. Lacking electrical cooling technology, the first innovations were facile attempts: some had legs, others lids, and a few even had crude selecting mechanisms. The first to garner any serious attention was the Icy-O, a tabletop model resembling a washing machine. With it, customers could view the bottles by turning a top-mounted crank. Inside, a rotating drum divided into quarters was filled with ice and water.

In 1928, the vending of bottled beverages gained its most ardent booster when Turner Jones, vice-president of Coca-Cola advertising, was inspired to produce a better cooler. Convinced that a practical device would get soda pop "out of the back rooms and dark corners and raise it to prominence," he called on engineer John Staton to construct a prototype. At company headquarters, Staton gathered up all the coolers on the market and tore them apart, studying their strengths, discovering their weaknesses, and devising plans to improve upon their design.

Six months later, he emerged from his work-shop with a rugged hybrid of the best configurations. To inhibit the chance of rust, metal sheeting that formed the heavily insulated cooling

The Seven-Up deliveryman in store, circa 1930s
Seven-Up was a prominent fixture in many grocery and drugstores during the 1930s through the 1950s. Long before Sprite and the current crop of citrus drinks usurped its rightful place in the hierarchy of uncolas, Seven-Up was the clear winner. How could consumers resist? After all, not all carbonated beverages dared make the claim that "It Likes You!" *Courtesy of the Dr Pepper Museum, Waco, Texas*

Coca-Cola machine, 1948
Vending machines were not only a great way to market Coca-Cola along North America's highways and byways, but a perfect outlet for the sale of carbonated cola drinks to the nation's workers. This 1948 advertisement depicts a Vendo Model V-83, which was made during the mid-1940s and 1950s. This was Vendo's first mass-produced upright coin-operated machine, a refrigerated, sealed unit capable of holding eighty-three bottles and pre-cooling seventy-five. *Author's Collection*

box was galvanized. All external nuts and bolts that might come into contact with water and the weather were plated as well. Capping the four feet, swiveling casters were added to provide portability. For the lid section on the top of the box, two metal panels that could be raised up independently with handles were hinged in the middle to form a unique butterfly-style arrangement.

Based on the prediction that fifteen thousand merchants would purchase them (at cost), Coca-Cola established a wholesale price of $12.50 for the standard model. Since the competing Icy-O unit sold for the considerable sum of $90 and was going out of production, the price was a genuine bargain. Forthwith, the Glasscock Brothers Manufacturing Company in Muncie, Indiana, was contracted to build the new cooler and refine it into a presentable product.

The newly manufactured cooler debuted at the 1929 bottlers convention. Decked out in a shiny red finish and green trim, it caught the gaze of attendees searching for practical retailing equipment. Bright red Coca-Cola signs were mounted on all four sides with the words "Serve Yourself" and "Please Pay the Clerk" added to the front and rear panels. Underneath, a sturdy shelf allowed dealers to store four yellow crates of Coke bottles where customers could see them. An affordable marketing device and a spectacular point-of-sale advertisement, the new cooler sold more than thirty thousand units the first year.

One year later, a mechanically refrigerated version of the Glasscock unit was developed, superseding models that required manual icing. As refrigeration became more affordable and compact, most of the major manufacturers modified existing cabinets to accommodate the new technology. When a coin-operated mechanism was added to the equation in 1932,

the era of the vending machine had officially begun. Suddenly, the silent salesmen were dispensing carbonated commodities at filling stations, motels, souvenir shops, grocery stores, movie theaters, and hot dog stands along roadside America.

As more manufacturers jumped into the burgeoning vending market, it was no longer enough for a soda machine to be a merely functional device. With all of the new competition for customers (of both the drinks and the machines), the qualities of overall beauty and external aesthetics became dominant design factors. Over the next two decades, vending machines were transformed into veritable works of art.

The mechanical beauty contest reached its zenith during the 1950s when industrial designers began taking decorative cues from the latest automobiles. By then, state-of-the-art styling included heavy trimwork, chrome plating, ribbed escutcheon panels, mirror-finish paint schemes, and curvaceous cabinetry. Established manufacturers like Artkraft, Cavalier, Mills, Vendo, Vendorlater, Westinghouse, and Quikold offered a line of fantastic sales robots that made the public's eyes pop.

By the end of the fifties, the soda machine joined the gas pump and traffic signal as an icon of the American roadside. Cars and carbonation became a popular combination, and the act of wetting one's whistle ensconced itself as a ritual of every motoring trip. Back then, there was nothing that matched the thrill of plunking a nickel down into a tiny slot, raising up the lid on a colorful cooler, reaching inside, grabbing a dripping bottle of pop from an icy reservoir of water, releasing the top on a sticky opener, raising it up to your lips, and chugging down its refreshing contents in one long, happy, greedy gulp.

Assortment of soda machines

Along the travel corridors of North America, the round corners, gleaming handles, and funny access doors of the classic soda vending machines have been replaced by brightly lit behemoths sporting money changers. Following the impersonal lead of modern roadside architecture, the vending machines of present day have evolved into a bland shadow of their former selves. These days, those mechanized salesmen of soda are devoid of all charm and character. *Courtesy of Rick Sweeney/CoolStock*

Ted Williams promotions, circa 1950s
Right: Boston Red Sox great Ted Williams signed a five-year promotional contract with the Moxie Company during the mid-1950s. Ted's image was used on billboard and point-of-purchase displays and also appeared on a special product called Ted's Creamy Root Beer. For forty-eight Moxie bottle caps, a kid could get a Ted Williams baseball—with a stamped autograph! *Courtesy of Frank Potter*

"Happy Homes have Nesbitt's," circa 1950s
Left: Nesbitt's used to be top of the pops when it came to orange-flavored refreshment. During the early 1950s, ads capitalized on the theme of entertainment—the kind that was right there in your living room on the TV screen. To keep the kids at bay, all a modern mom needed was a well-stocked Frigidaire full of soda drinks and a Zenith console. Nesbitt's was a franchised drink first bottled in 1924 by Nesbitt's Fruit Products, Inc. of Los Angeles, California. *Author's Collection*

I like Ike, and Ike likes Coke, 1950s
Above: During Dwight D. Eisenhower's term as the thirty-fourth President of the United States, the world saw the end of the Korean War, the U.S. Supreme Court rule against racial segregation, the launch of the first space satellite, the inauguration of jet passenger service, the first atomic power plant, and the completion of the St. Lawrence Seaway. During it all, the formula for Coca-Cola remained the same, and public demand never waned. *Courtesy of The Coca-Cola Company*

Backyard barbecue ad, *Ladies Home Journal,* 1951
Left, top: Bottles of carbonated soft drink slowly found their way into the refrigerators of families, and by the end of the 1950s, images like this one were splashed upon the pages of most every major magazine. Cowboys and Indians, the backyard barbecue, picnics, a log-cabin playhouse, and extra leisure time were all potent images to sell the good life to thirsty consumers. *Author's Collection*

"Winter Warmer" ad, 1965
Left, bottom: Among Dr Pepper President Wesby Parker's innovations: hot Dr Pepper! Parker got the idea when he visited a bottler during a blizzard who commented that a hot drink would be nice. Parker pondered the possibilities and experimented. He found that heating Dr Pepper (without scalding it) provided the best flavor. To make it perfect, he also specified that a lemon slice—not lemon juice—be added to the mug. Advertising during the late 1950s through the mid-1960s promoted the idea as both a wintertime and holiday treat. *Author's Collection*

Nu-Grape Soda clock, 1960s

Above: Nu-Grape followed the lead of the major soda makers and produced a number of dealer premiums. During the 1960s, many retail stores were adorned with cool timepieces like this one, reminding customers that it was time to down a cold bottle of Nu-Grape. Nu-Grape was born at the Kelly Brothers bottling plant in Atlanta, Georgia, in 1920. One year later, the Nu-Grape Company of America was formed to franchise bottlers and market the drink. *Author/Clock courtesy Clare and Helen Patterson Jr.*

Dad's Root Beer sign, circa 1960s

Right: Dad's Old Fashioned Root Beer debuted in 1937, bottled by the Monarch Company of Atlanta, Georgia. In those days, advertising still relied heavily on signs that were affixed to the front of drugstores and general sundry suppliers. Made of pressed tin and sometimes of weatherproof, porcelain-enameled steel, these durable ads have survived into the present day and are enthusiastically hoarded by today's sign collectors. Dad's is still going strong today. *Author*

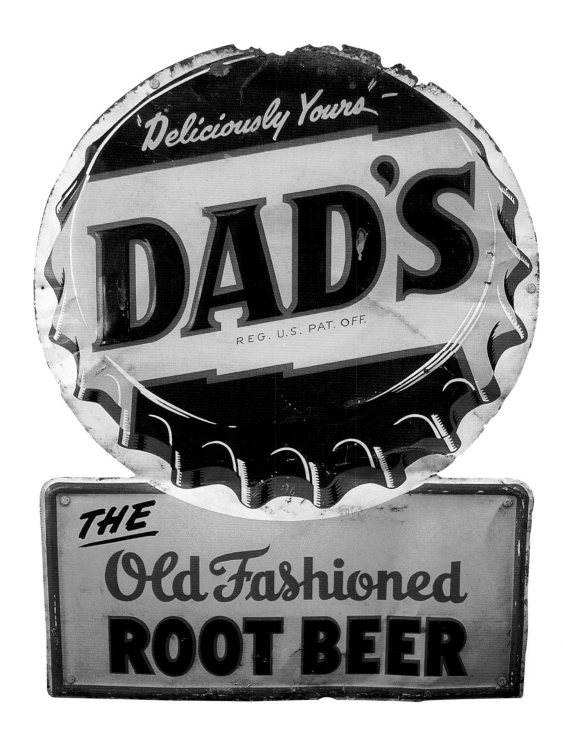

"Dodger Tastes Good," circa 1960s

Dodger was another one of those short-lived wonders of the soda pop world. For a brief period during the 1960s, people just couldn't get enough of Dodger, and then, just as quickly as it had appeared, it slipped into relative obscurity. *Preziosi Postcards*

Dr Pepper "candy-striped" containers, late 1950s

Above: Dr Pepper experimented with a multicolor candy-stripe design for its bottles and cans at the end of the 1950s. Curious as it was, the slogan "frosty man, frosty" accompanied the familiar "10-2-4" on the new containers. Although this festive packaging was intended only for a limited test market and was short-lived, a companion St. Bernard mascot with the name "Frosty" won favor with young customers. *Author/Dr Pepper Museum, Waco, Texas*

Old Faithful and Oregon Trail bottles, circa 1960s

Left: Applied-color-label bottles like these Old Faithful (circa 1964, bottled in Idaho Falls, Idaho) and Oregon Trail beauties (date unknown, bottled in Alliance, Nebraska) have emerged as hot collectibles. Today, if it's a rare brand and has a cool graphic or name on it, bottle collectors the world over will want to display it on their shelves. *Courtesy of Rick Sweeney*

Kickapoo Joy Juice, circa 1967

Introduced in 1967 by the Monarch Company of Atlanta, Georgia, Kickapoo Joy Juice was one of those strange novelty flavors that saw only a limited regional success. Now defunct, the brand employed both Native American and prehistoric stereotypes to sell the syrup. While this aging jug is way past its prime, it's a valuable reminder of yesterday's funny flavors and the whimsy of pop. *Author/Dr Pepper Bottling Company of Dublin*

Coca-Cola Harley-Davidson tour, 1996

"Time to Refuel . . . with Real Cola Taste" was the slogan for a cross-country Coca-Cola promotional tour in 1996. As part of the tour, a caravan of two support vehicles carried promotional drink coolers and three Harley-Davidson motorcycles equipped with specially built Coca-Cola bottle sidecars. At select supermarkets, both the cycles and drinks were unloaded and put on display. Patrons received free bottles of Coca-Cola and a chance to drool over the outrageous two-wheelers as they were driven into position by a trio of lucky lads. *Author*

"Fanta takes off" ad

With expectations for big business, Coca-Cola bottling operations were at work in Germany as early as 1929. Unfortunately, beer-loving Germans preferred their traditional brews to the sweet beverage. In 1933, Max Keith went to work for the European bottling plant and introduced ice cold Coca-Cola by passing out sample bottles to taverns. During World War II, ingredients could no longer be shipped in, so Coca-Cola production stopped. As a result, Keith developed an entirely new soda pop he called Fanta, a light-colored drink that resembled ginger ale. The Fanta line of carbonated fruit drinks are still extremely popular in Europe today. *Courtesy of The Coca-Cola Company*

Coca-Cola water tower, 1990s

Coca-Cola is one soda pop that enjoys fame and fortune around the globe—and is sometimes easier to find than safe drinking water, as symbolized by this water storage tank in Nogales, Mexico. *Author*

"Always Cool," 1990s

During the "Always Coca-Cola" campaign of the 1990s, TV ads for Coca-Cola depicted computer-generated polar bears enjoying the beverage. Although the animated images were striking, the concept behind them was by no means new. Not known by the company at the time, a commercial artist had already experimented with the bear-and-bottle image in 1920s Paris. In that version, the polar bears standing on hind legs fed the sun a cold bottle of Coca-Cola. *Courtesy of The Coca-Cola Company*

Pepsi billboard in Seattle, 1989

By the late 1940s, the rising cost of ingredients required to make Pepsi dictated a new sales policy. To entice consumers, "Twice as Much for a Penny More" was adopted as the new slogan. Unfortunately, the revised message never caught on. By decade's end, the "Bigger is Better" concept died. On cue, the exuberance of the 1950s ushered in an entirely new catch-phrase geared toward the svelte, active, and vibrant woman. "The Light Refreshment" that "refreshes without filling" had arrived. As cars grew tailfins and appendages of chrome, the idea of saving money was out and the notion of refreshing taste in. Pepsi was a juggernaut heading into the future of pop culture. This neon wonder was photographed in Seattle, Washington. *Author*

Bibliography

Allen, Frederick. *Secret Formula*. New York: HarperCollins Publishers, Inc., 1994.

Armstrong, David and Elizabeth Metzger Armstrong. *The Great American Medicine Show*. New York: Prentice Hall, 1991.

Brody, Jane E. "Good News About Coffee." *New York Times*, reprinted in *Reader's Digest* (September 1996): 141-144.

Brown, Dr. O. Phelps. *The Complete Herbalist*. North Hollywood, California: Newcastle Publishing, 1993.

Brown, John Hull. *Early American Beverages*. Rutland, Vermont: Charles. E. Tuttle Company, 1966.

Cadbury Schweppes Public Limited Company. *Cadbury Schweppes Fact Sheets*. London, England: Cadbury Schweppes, 1995.

Calhoun, Mary. *Medicine Show: Conning People and Making Them Like It*. New York: Harper & Row, Publishers, 1976.

Carson, Gerald. *One for a Man, Two for a Horse*. New York: Bramhall House, [n.d.].

Cash, G. Howard. *All In Flavour: The Canadian Soft Drink Industry and Its Association 1942–1992*. Toronto: The Canadian Soft Drink Association, 1992.

Coon, Nelson. *Using Plants for Healing*. Emmaus, Pennsylvania: Roadal Press, 1963.

Datkso, Jim. "Hey Dad! Can we Have a Bottle of Pop? Please?" *Route 66 Magazine* (Winter 1996): 50-51.

Day, Avanelle and Lillie Stuckey. *The Spice Cookbook*. New York: David White Company, 1964.

Deogun, Nikhil. "Coke to Test Curvy Can in South, Midwest." *Wall Street Journal* (February 6, 1997): B1, B9.

Dickson, Paul. *The Great American Ice Cream Book*. New York: Galahad Books, 1972.

Dietz, Lawrence. *Soda Pop: The History, Advertising, Art and Memorabilia of Soft Drinks in America*. New York: Simon and Schuster, 1973.

Dorsey, Leslie and Devine Janice. *Fare Thee Well: A Backward Look at Two Centuries of Historic American Hostelries, Fashionable Spas, and Seaside Resorts*. New York : Crown Publishers, 1964.

"Dublin Dr Pepper Reaches Century; Birthday Party Attracts Thousands." *Mid-Continent Bottler*, Vol. 45, No. 3 (June-July 1991): 12-14.

"Dublin Dr. Pepper Plant Completely Modernized." *Dr Pepper Clock Dial Magazine*. (May-June 1951): 16.

"Dublin Plant Reviews 64-Year Progress." *Dr. Pepper Clock Dial Magazine*. (September-October 1955).

Dwyer, Brian. "1890's Great Gas Controversy." *Poor Richard's Saratoga Journal* (July 1996): Cover, 23, 33.

Ebert, Albert Ethelbert, Ph.D. and A. Emil Hiss, Ph.G. *The Standard Formulary: A Collection of Over Four Thousand Formulas*. Chicago, Illinois: G. P. Englehard & Co., 1896.

Elling, Michael M. "Crown Cap Reveals Nehi Produced 'Nehi Cola'." *Soda Net: The Official Newsletter of the Painted Soda Bottle Collector's Association* (January 1991): 6-7.

Enrico, Roger and Jesse Kornbluth. *The Other Guy Blinked: How Pepsi Won the Cola Wars*. New York: Bantam Books, 1986.

Erlbach, Arlene. *Soda Pop: How It's Made*. Minneapolis, Minnesota: Lerner Publications Company, 1994.

Ferguson, Frank L. *Efficient Drug Store Management*. New York: Fairchild Publications, Inc., 1969.

Foner, Eric and John A. Garraty, editors. *The Reader's Companion to American History*. Boston, Massachussetts: Houghton Mifflin Company, 1991.

Foster, Steven and Yue Chongxi. *Herbal Emissaries*. Rochester, Vermont: Healing Arts Press, 1992.

Fowler, Gene. *Crazy Water*. Forth Worth, Texas: Texas Christian University Press, 1991.

Fowler, Ron. "Opening a Time Capsule." *Soda Net: The Official Newsletter of the Painted Soda Bottle Collector's Association* (March 1991): 6-12.

Funderburg, Ann Cooper. *Chocolate, Strawberry, and Vanilla: A History of American Ice Cream*. Bowling Green, Ohio: Bowling Green State University Press, 1995.

Furnell, Dennis. *Health from the Hedgerow*. London, England: B. T. Batsford Ltd., 1985.

Garraty, John A. *1,001 Things Everyone Should Know About American History*. New York: Doubleday, 1989.

Gazan, M. H. *Flavours and Essences*. London, England: Chapman & Hall Ltd., 1936.

Gomez, Linda. "Cocaine: America's 100 Years of Euphoria and Despair." *Life* (May 1984): 57-64.

Gordon, Liz. "Waco's Dr Pepper Museum Pays Homage to The Friendly Pepper-Upper." *Texas Highways*, Vol. 40, No. 7 (July 1993): 38-42.

Gordon, Liz. "It's Original." *Texas Highways*, Vol. 40, No. 7 (July 1993): 43-45.

Gordy, Wilbur Fisk. *History of the United States*. New York: Charles Scribner's Sons, 1932.

Grimes, William. *Straight Up or On the Rocks: A Cultural History of American Drink*. New York: Simon & Schuster, 1993.

Hechtlinger, Adelaide. *The Great Patent Medicine Era, or Without Benefit of Doctor*. New York: Grosset & Dunlap, Inc., 1970.

Hoy, Anne. *The First Hundred Years: Coca-Cola*. Atlanta, Georgia: The Coca-Cola Company, 1986.

Huckins, Kyle. "In Dublin, It's Just What The Doctor Ordered." *etc. The Magazine That Brings You More* (March 1996): 24-25.

"It's the Real Thing." *Spotlight*, Texas Utilities System (September 1990): 6-7.

Ivey, Mark. "Moving Up and Out." *Waco Tribune Herald* (December 2, 1979) .

Jacobs, Morris B., Ph.D. *Synthetic Food Adjuncts*. New York: D. Van Nostrand Company, Inc., 1947.

John R. Paul, Paul W. Parmalee. *Soft Drink Bottling, A History with Special Reference to Illinois*. Springfield, Illinois: Illinois State Museum Society, 1973.

Kestner, Laura. "Former Soda Jerk Recalls 'Wacos' and Curb Service." *The Dublin Citizen* (August 3, 1995).

Kremers, Edward. *Kremers' and Urdang's History of Pharmacy*. Philadelphia, Pennsylvania: Lippincott, 1976.

LaCroix, Paul C. *The Cliquot Club Company*. Unpublished manuscript, 1995.

Langdon, Philip. *Orange Roofs, Golden Arches*. New

York: Alfred A. Knopf, Inc., 1986.

Lloyd, Everette and Mary Lloyd. *Pepsi-Cola Collectibles, With Price Guide*. Atglen, Pennsylvania: Schiffer Publishing Ltd., 1993.

Lofland, Cheryl Harris. *The National Soft Drink Association: A Tradition of Service*. Washington, D.C.: National Soft Drink Association, 1986.

Mack, Walter with Peter Buckley. *No Time Lost*. New York: Atheneum, 1982.

Marsh, Thomas. *The Official Guide to Collecting Applied Color Label Soda Bottles*. Youngstown, Ohio: Thomas E. Marsh, Inc., 1992.

Martin, Milward W. *Twelve Full Ounces*. New York: Holt, Rinehart and Winston, 1969.

Mayo, P. Randolph, Jr. *Coca-Cola Heritage*. Austin, Texas: Best Printing Company, Inc., 1990.

McCullough, William. "Keeping the Record Straight: The True Story of Dr Pepper." Unpublished letter written by early associate of R. S. Lazenby.

McCutheon, Marc. *Everyday Life in the 1800's*. Cincinnati, Ohio: Writer's Digest Books, 1993.

Merory, Joseph. *Food Flavorings: Composition, Manufacture, and Use*. Westport, Connecticut: The AVI Publishing Company, Inc., 1960.

Moore, Roy. W. *Down From Canada Came Tales of a Wonderful Beverage*. New York: Newcomen Society, 1961.

Morrison, Tom. *Root Beer: Advertising and Collectibles*. West Chester, Pennsylvania: Schiffer Publishing, 1992.

Morthland, John. "Wouldn't You Like to Be a Pepper Too?" *Texas Monthly*, Vol. 18, No. 5 (May 1990): 106–107.

Mowrey, Daniel B., Ph.D. *The Scientific Validation of Herbal Medicine*. Cormorant Books, 1986.

Munsey, Cecil. *The Illustrated Guide to the Collectibles of Coca-Cola*. New York: Hawthorn Books, Inc., 1972.

"Old Doc's Soda Shop to Open its Doors Saturday." *The Dublin Citizen* (August 3, 1995).

Oliver, Thomas. *The Real Coke, The Real Story*. New York: Random House, 1986.

Palazzini, Fiora Steinbach. *Coca-Cola Superstar*. New York: Barron's Educational Series, 1989.

Pepsi-Cola Company. "History and Milestones." Various company historical fact sheets, published 1995.

Pepsi-Cola Company. "Pepsi-Cola Advertising Timeline." Various company historical fact sheets, published by PepsiCo Inc., 1995.

Petretti, Alan. *Petretti's Coca-Cola Collectibles Price Guide, The Encyclopedia of Coca-Cola Collectibles*. Radnor, Pennsylvania: Wallace Homestead, 1992.

Petroski, Henry. "Form Follows Failure." *American Heritage of Invention & Technology*, Vol 8, No. 2, (Fall 1992): 54–61.

Phillis Shimko. *Sarsaparilla Bottle Encyclopedia*. Oregon: Andrew & Phyllis Shimko, 1969.

Pomeroy, Ralph. *The Ice Cream Connection*. New York: Paddington Press Ltd., Two Continents Publishing Group, 1975.

Potter, Frank N. *The Book of Moxie*. Paducah, Kentucky: Collector Books, 1987.

Potter, Frank N. *The Moxie Mystique*. Paducah, Kentucky: Moxiebooks, 1981.

Poundstone, William. *Big Secrets*. New York: William Morrow and Company, Inc., 1983.

Rawcliffe, Carole. *Medicine & Society in Later Medieval England*. United Kingdom: Alan Sutton Publishing Limited, 1995.

"Red Letter Days In Big Red's Past." *Big Red Ink*, Vol. 1, No. 1, (Spring 1984): 1.

Riley, John J. *A History of the American Soft Drink Industry*. Washington, D.C.: American Bottlers of Carbonated Beverages, 1958.

Rodengen, Jefferey L. *The Legend of Dr Pepper/Seven-Up*. Ft. Lauderdale, Florida: Write Stuff Syndicate, Inc., 1995.

Royal Crown Company, Inc. "Company History." Unpublished article. Ft. Lauderdale: Florida (1994).

Sachorow, Stanley. *Symbols of Trade*. New York: Art Direction Book Company, 1982.

Shih, Ko Ching, Ph.D., and C. Ying Shih, Ph.D. *American Soft Drink Industry and the Carbonated Beverage Market*. Brookfield, Wisconsin: W. A. Krueger Co., 1965.

Simmons, Douglas A. *Schweppes: The First 200 Years*. Washington, D.C.: Acropolis Books, 1983.

Swanner, Grace Maguire, M.D. *Saratoga Queen of Spas*. Utica, New York: North Country Books, Inc., 1988.

Tchudi, Stephen N. *Soda Poppery: The History of Soft Drinks in America*. New York: Charles Scribner's Sons, 1986.

Time-Life Books, by the Editors. *This Fabulous Century: Prelude 1870–1900*. New York: Time-Life Books, 1970.

Triarc Companies, Inc. "A Progress Report, 1994."

Company Progress Report, published 1994.

Tufts, James W. *The Manufacturing and Bottling of Carbonated Beverages*. Fort Davis, Texas: Frontier Book Company, 1969.

Vaughn, Glenn. "The Fizz and Fizzle of Royal Crown: Georgia's Other Cola." *Georgia Trend*, Vol. 10, No. 10 (June 1995): 28–36.

Vaughn, Glenn. "The RC Cola Story: Part Two, Royal Crown Fights Back With Old Weapon: New Product." *Georgia Trend*, (July 1995): 56–58, 60.

Vaughn, Glenn. "What Makes Colas Most Popular Drink? Taste and Promotion." *Georgia Trend*, (July 1995): 59.

Vehling, Bill and Michael Hunt. *Pepsi-Cola Collectibles*. Gas City, Indiana: L-W Books Sales, 1986.

Walker, Mildred. *Crown Cork & Seal Co., Inc*. Unpublished, undated manuscript.

Walker, Mildred. *Soft Drinks and Their Owners/Franchisers*. Unpublished, undated manuscript.

Walter, Erich. *Manual for the Essence Industry*. New York: John Wiley & Sons, Inc., 1916.

Walters, Jeff. *Classic Soda Machines, A Field Reference and Price Guide*. Pollock Pines, California: Memory Lane, 1992.

"Watering Places." *Heritage*, Vol. 1, No. 5 (May-June 1985): 12–20.

Watkins. T. H. *The Great Depression*. New York: Little, Brown and Company, 1993.

Watters, Pat. *Coca-Cola: An Illustrated History*. Garden City, New York: Doubleday & Company, Inc., 1978.

Weaver, A. F. *Book of Programs*. Unpublished manuscript, 1996.

Weaver, A. F. *Time Was In Mineral Wells*. Mineral Wells, Texas: A. F. Weaver, 1988.

Witzel, Michael Karl. *Drive-In Deluxe*. Osceola, Wisconsin: Motorbooks International, 1997.

Witzel, Michael Karl. *The American Drive-In: History and Folklore of the Drive-In Restaurant in American Car Culture*. Osceola, Wisconsin: Motorbooks International, 1994.

Woolley, Bryan. "Where the Fizz Is." *Dallas Life Magazine* (September 29, 1991): 8–9.

Wunderlich, Keith D. *Deliciously Different: The Vernor's Ginger Ale Story*. Unpublished manuscript, 1996.

Young, James Harvey. *The Toadstool Millionaires: A Social History of Patent Medicines in America Before Federal Regulation*. Princeton, New Jersey: Princeton University Press, 1961.

Index

About the Authors

Michael Karl Witzel is an award-winning author and photographer. His published works include *The American Gas Station*, *Gas Station Memories*, *The American Drive-In*, *Drive-In Deluxe*, *Route 66 Remembered*, and *Cruisin.* His nostalgic column on Roadside America appears monthly in *Mobilia* magazine.

Gyvel Young-Witzel conducts historical research (and has done so for many of the non-fiction titles above) and also finds the time to pursue her own writing career—her first screenplay is in the works. She is the author of a humorous cat book, *Meows: I Want It and I Shall Have It*, and has penned a number of articles for the magazine trade, including *Chickadee* and *Horseman* magazines.

Along with two feline writing companions (Spunky and Zeppelin), the authors battle the winds in the Tornado Alley area of Kansas with their Australian Shepherd, Smylee.